PRAISE FOR *AUTHENTIC NEGOTIATING*

"*Authentic Negotiating* is simply fantastic! Corey understands negotiating at a level that few others do. I recently hired him to structure and negotiate a very important deal for me and was thrilled with the refreshingly authentic process and the results. If you buy this book, you will be as well!"

> —**DAVID BACH,** *nine-time* New York Times *best-selling author* of Start Late Finish Rich *and* The Automatic Millionaire, *founder* of FinishRich.com.

"Negotiation is a key part of my life and has been for the past twelve years, as I have done fifteen M&A transactions for our family and advised on over two hundred for clients. Corey gives us great insight and practical ideas on negotiation strategy and tools that readers can implement to help them in not just business but all aspects of life. "

> —**JOHN BLY,** *CPA, CVA, CM&AA, CGMA, co-managing member of LBA Haynes Strand, PLLC, author of* Cracking the Code: An Entrepreneur's Guide to Growing your Business through Mergers and Acquisitions for Pennies on the Dollar

"*Authentic Negotiating* is a groundbreaking book and an absolute must-read for women. Negotiating is a key skill from which we too often shy away and which significantly impacts our ability to build wealth and achieve other goals. Corey brilliantly guides us through an internal journey of self-awareness and provides insights, frameworks, and tools that are authentic, practical, and highly effective. I recommend his book to any woman who desires financial success!"

—**BARBARA STANNY,** *leading authority on women and money, motivational speaker, financial educator, and author of* Prince Charming Isn't Coming: How Women Get Smart about Money *and* Secrets of Six-Figure Women

"This inspiring book shows you exactly how to maintain business relationships, stay true to yourself, and achieve your objectives. *Authentic Negotiating* is the negotiating book for our times—people will be studying and applying this for decades to come. Must read!"

—**DAVE KERPEN,** New York Times *best-selling author of* The Art of People, *CEO of Likeable Local*

"Negotiation is a critical skill in business. Yet most people never master the art and end up losing hundreds of thousands and even millions over the course of their careers. As a clinical psychologist, I've read several books and been through two, multiday, high-level training programs on negotiating, but I learned more about the discipline and science of negotiation in this book than anything I've done before. Far beyond simplistic techniques and mere manipulation, Kupfer goes into the depths of strategy and creates a compelling framework that will educate and train even the most experienced negotiators."

—**STEPHEN FAIRLEY,** CEO of the Rainmaker Institute, international best-selling author of twelve books

"Corey's ability to combine practical, experience-based negotiating wisdom, with a deep understanding of the internal work required for authentic success, makes *Authentic Negotiating* a must-read book!"

—**JOHN ASSARAF,** serial entrepreneur, brain researcher, CEO of NeuroGym, author of two New York Times best-selling books, Having It All and The Answer

"Corey Kupfer's *Authentic Negotiating* is a great book; its message really resonated with me, and I expect it will with anyone who negotiates for a living. Corey's unique approach, which I have seen in action in deals we have done together, is honest, refreshing, and rooted in integrity. It works! Buy the book and become a master at negotiating—one of the key skills in closing the deals you are meant to."

—MINDY DIAMOND, *president and CEO of Diamond Consultants, a leading executive search and consulting firm, guiding financial advisors to find their best business life*

"If M&A negotiations are a complex, emotional roller coaster to an unknown destination, then *Authentic Negotiating* is the equivalent of Dramamine and a topographical map of the territory. As someone who has worked with Corey on a wide number of transactions over the last decade, I can personally attest to his knowledge of the subject and negotiating acumen. This guide should be required reading for any business owner contemplating a merger, sale, or acquisition."

—DAVID DEVOE, *managing partner of DeVoe & Company, an investment bank and management consulting firm serving the wealth management and investment management industries*

"*Authentic Negotiating* is a brilliant book with crucial information for entrepreneurs and executives who want to grow their companies. Applying its principles, Corey has successfully negotiated and closed significant deals for me including the recent sale and merger of my advisory firms. I recommend the book without hesitation!"

—**AJAY GUPTA,** *chief investment strategist, Creative Planning, Inc., featured in Tony Robbins* New York Times *best-selling book* Money: Master the Game: 7 Simple Steps to Financial Freedom

"Having built six companies into national firms, I sure wish Corey had written this book sooner. The unique insights and practical approaches would have been worth millions of dollars. Read it and reap!"

—**JACK DALY,** *professional sales coach, speaker, expert in corporate culture, and Amazon best-selling author of* Hyper Sales Growth

"Corey Kupfer is a gift, as are his ideas, spoken and written. I met Corey over twenty years ago on a TV show regarding entrepreneurship, where he demonstrated the spirit of an entrepreneur and the rigor of an attorney. He has been both a client and my own attorney, and I've watched him take real risk in his personal life, community life, and professional life to develop his vision and to explore the cutting edges of where he can contribute most. These risks have included ending world hunger, 'awakening' men, and interrupting racial bias.

He is a leader who can operate at both the level of details and vision. Corey brings the power of flexible, creative thinking to negotiation and, for that matter, all his human interactions. For Corey, 'win-win' isn't a joke—it's a way of life. Get to know Corey Kupfer; read his book and take him on."

—ANTHONY M. SMITH, CEO, VSA Consulting Group, LLC

"Negotiating can bring up a lot of fear and discomfort for people. In his book, Authentic Negotiating, Corey Kupfer demystifies the process and even makes it fun! He's based his negotiating frameworks and tools on universal spiritual principals but has still kept it extremely practical. This book will give you the confidence to go after what you want and trust your intuition along the way!"

—GABRIELLE BERNSTEIN, international speaker and number-one New York Times bestselling author of The Universe Has Your Back

AUTHENTIC
NEGOTIATING

AUTHENTIC
NEGOTIATING

CLARITY, DETACHMENT, & EQUILIBRIUM

THE THREE KEYS TO TRUE NEGOTIATING

SUCCESS & HOW TO ACHIEVE THEM

COREY KUPFER

Published by Advantage, Charleston, South Carolina.
Member of Advantage Media Group.

ADVANTAGE is a registered trademark, and the Advantage colophon is a trademark of Advantage Media Group, Inc.

Printed in the United States of America.

ISBN: 978-1-59932-595-8
LCCN: 2016960377

Cover design by Katie Biondo.

This publication is designed to provide accurate and authoritative information in regard to the subject matter covered. It is sold with the understanding that the publisher is not engaged in rendering legal, accounting, or other professional services. If legal advice or other expert assistance is required, the services of a competent professional person should be sought.

Some names and identifying details used in this book have been changed to protect the privacy of individuals.

Advantage Media Group is proud to be a part of the Tree Neutral® program. Tree Neutral offsets the number of trees consumed in the production and printing of this book by taking proactive steps such as planting trees in direct proportion to the number of trees used to print books. To learn more about Tree Neutral, please visit **www.treeneutral.com.**

Advantage Media Group is a publisher of business, self-improvement, and professional development books. We help entrepreneurs, business leaders, and professionals share their Stories, Passion, and Knowledge to help others Learn & Grow. Do you have a manuscript or book idea that you would like us to consider for publishing? Please visit **advantagefamily.com** or call **1.866.775.1696.**

This book is dedicated to my father, Howard Kupfer, who passed away just before the first draft of this book was completed. The world was blessed to have him for eighty years. He taught me many lessons (several of which I share at www.coreykupfer.com), and he still inspires me every day.

TABLE OF CONTENTS

FOREWORD

uthentic Negotiating, by author Corey Kupfer, gives us new ideas about an age-old process. Negotiation is something that each of us uses virtually every day of our lives, and yet, few truly understand its nuances or significance. It is so commonly used that we fail to recognize we are doing it and most often don't understand its consequences or importance. Corey has used his personal experiences, as a lawyer and businessman, to enable us to better understand the importance of negotiation, the role it plays in our lives, and how we can be most effective in our role as a negotiator. Whatever activity we engage in, we frequently find ourselves in that role. The circumstance can be in the family, business, or community or for ourselves. Having the vision, mind-set, and tools to enable one to reach the desired outcomes of any negotiation is essential for success.

For business executives and entrepreneurs, becoming a great negotiator is one of the best things they can do to further their success and the success of their companies. During my career, I have served as CEO or chairman of seventeen companies and on the board of directors for fifty public, private, and nonprofit organizations. I have also had the honor of being a White House Fellow, Appointments Secretary and Cabinet Secretary to President Ford, international chairman of the World Presidents Organization (WPO) and of L3, and founder and Dean of Faculty at the Entrepreneurs' Organization's (EO) Leadership Academy. I have studied business and entrepreneurial and life success and now focus my life to supporting leaders, especially those committed to having an impact in the world. My experience getting to know Corey started when he was president of the New York chapter of Entrepreneurs' Organization and a member of the EO Leadership Academy. He is a leader, a deep thinker, a strong communicator, and someone committed to being of service and inspiring authenticity in business. He also understands what it takes to attain true negotiating success in a way that few do.

For many people, negotiation is a zero-sum game of win or lose or something they think they need to approach from a place that does not align with their values and inner truth. Corey helps us understand that it is much more than that and that you can stay aligned and be authentic. In fact, doing so is the best path to true negotiating success. Using what he calls CDE, or Clarity, Detachment, and Equilibrium, he teaches you to find new spaces and new ways in which to negotiate fairly, authentically, and successfully. These principles support a combination of self-awareness, self-knowledge, inner truth, and depth of preparation that are crucial in obtaining and maintaining clarity; supporting you in becoming emotionally detached from the process itself, so you can walk calmly away from the transaction if you achieve your objectives; and maintaining your equilibrium, balance, emotional composure, and stability during the course of debate and discussions. These things, which few focus on and many fail to master, are necessary to achieve great things through negotiations.

I have spent the better part of my life in situations where being a good negotiator was necessary to determine my future and the success I would ultimately have. I believe this book, *Authentic Negotiating,* will give you wonderful new insight, ideas, and principles on which you can base your future negotiations. You will find new ways to secure the outcomes you desire while maintaining your values and integrity.

This is a book that will add value to your entire life.

—**WARREN RUSTAND,** CEO Tycon, Inc. and former CEO of Providence Service Corporation, Rural Metro Corporation, and TLC Vision

ACKNOWLEDGMENTS

So many people made this book possible, supported me in life and business, and shared their wisdom and life experiences and encouraged me to share mine.

- First and foremost, my wife, Rha Goddess, who is my soul mate and biggest champion.
- My mother, Cecille Kupfer, and my father (to whom this book is dedicated) who are my biggest teachers and mentors.
- My brother, Douglas, who is always there for me when I need him, and my sister-in-law, Jean, and nephews, Matthew, Benjamin, and Ethan, who bring me such joy in my life.
- My local and regional Entrepreneurs' Organization forummates (Allen, Fernando, Eddy, Dan, Veeral, Raj, Jane, Paul, Vijay, Jen, Dan, Chuck, and Scott), who support, challenge, and hold me accountable to be my best self.
- All of my EO, National Speaker Association, and Social Venture Network fellow members and board members, who, more than most, understand the journey I am on.
- My brother from another mother, Richard Levychin, who is always causing trouble for my own good.
- The many great personal, spiritual, and business growth teachers, including Bob Proctor, Wallace D. Wattles, Tony Robbins, Wayne Dyer, Jack Canfield, and so many other individuals and organization that have supported my lifelong learning and growth—your teachings are a large part of who I am today.

- My many mentors and coaches in business and life—including, specifically, my first business coach, friend, and client, Tony Smith—who have pushed me to higher levels of understanding, success, accountability, and service.

- So many colleagues and business partners with whom I have worked along the way and who continue to make a difference in my life, including Jon Tota, who is my friend, client, and Authentic Negotiating online course partner.

- My entire Kupfer & Associates and Authentic Enterprises teams, including Dawn Hertzel, BeeSian Yap, Arnie Herz, and Dan Shlufman, who just get it done and are driven to serve.

- Every one of our great clients, who have put their trust in us for so many years.

- All of the readers of my book manuscript and the countless people who gave input on the cover design, including Rha, Allen Frechter, Raj Thakkar, Gael Bevan, Jen Sterling, and Fi Jamieson-Folland, who gave me detailed input on the manuscript. This book is better because of all of you.

I am so blessed to have so many good friends—too many to individually list—from all over the world. They include friends from so many communities, geographies, and stages in my life; the great friends I have met through Rha; all of the clients and business associates who have become good friends; and my college buddies.

INTRODUCTION

Thirty years ago, I witnessed a man stay calm in the midst of high tension and drama during a $150M leveraged buyout negotiation. (You will read about Mike and that negotiation in chapter 1.) Ever since then, I have been trying to figure out what Mike knew—what he understood that allowed him to be the calm in the eye of the negotiating storm.

My drive to figure this out stemmed not only from a desire to be successful and help others to be successful but also from my inherent curiosity of what it means to be authentic—to stay true to who we are while achieving the results we want. I have seen many people achieve the trappings of success but not be happy. After spending time in villages in Ghana, Uganda, and India and experiencing people with so little but who have so much joy and sense of connection, I redefined myself as a world citizen connected to all of humanity but also experienced and occasionally engaged in transactional and manipulative interactions in business, life, and negotiations.

I have seen the adverse impact that the need to win has on others—and on those who have that need—and the deep corrosiveness of ego, anger, fear, and manipulation on people's souls. I have come to understand that, as the great Wallace Wattles teaches, operating on the creative plane is a much higher state of being and brings much more success and happiness than operating on the competitive plane.

From this, I developed some fundamental beliefs and a core framework for successful negotiating that is different from most of what was and is being taught about negotiating in many places—and that is what I will share with you in this book. If that seems like a leap for you, or you don't understand the connection between the life experiences I share and successful negotiation, I am confident that, once you read the book, you will understand.

This philosophy and approach has been the basis for great results for clients over the last three decades as a hired negotiator on everything from small to large corporate deals, to various types of disputes and other tough negotiating situations—mostly in the realm of business—and in negotiating my own deals for my various businesses by applying these principles. I have also used this philosophy and framework to help others deal with challenging circumstances, but the real test for me came in 2008. That test challenged me to the core of who I am, and I share that story at the end of the book.

This book is the culmination of my thirty-year journey of learning, application, and evolution; countless negotiations over that time; and a particularly challenging soul-searching test of character. That is how I know that if you practice and apply the teachings in this book, you will significantly increase your chances of being successful in any negotiating situation—and beyond.

CHAPTER ONE

MIKE THE MASTERFUL

The greatest single early influence in the development of my understanding of authentic negotiating was a man I met in 1984 when I was working as a summer associate between my second and third year of law school. I went to work for a firm at which a man named Mike was the head partner. Mike was a fairly well-known figure; he was regularly written up as one of the top fifty securities lawyers in the country. Coming in as a first-year associate, I was already in awe of him. I was young and hopeful that I'd make the cut and be asked back to work there when I graduated, so I paid close attention to how he and the other partners were doing things.

A lot of my time that summer was spent working on a leveraged buyout deal. The executive management team of a retail chain was buying the company from its owners, a father and son team, for $150 million. The management team had pooled their money and was borrowing most of the rest of the money from a major credit corporation, who was our client. That was the heyday of leveraged buyouts, and this was a typical highly leveraged deal of those times.

Even though our client, the credit corporation, was going to lend the management team most of the money, the team needed to put up a portion of the necessary funds; additionally, they were responsible for a list of expenses that had to be paid, regardless of whether or not the deal closed: the legal, accounting, investment banking, and other fees. Many of the team members had leveraged their homes and other personal assets to procure the money required to complete this deal. It had been negotiated over several months, and it all culminated on this one night, near midnight on a Thursday.

Picture the twelve of us sitting in a conference room in our Manhattan offices around a polished wooden table that seats twenty: the management team, the owners, the lenders, and the lawyers for each of these parties. The air was acrid with the stink of stale coffee, cigarette smoke, and the sour body odor of people who have been in the same room for almost fifteen hours. We were down to the last issues and the deal was falling apart. These management guys had put their collective financial lives on the line—and now their own lawyers' refusal to give a legal opinion as they'd agreed to do months earlier was about to derail everything. The deal was about to go down in flames and take the buyers with it.

"We're not giving that opinion, I don't care what we said," one of the lawyers for the management team kept repeating stubbornly. At this point, he was rapidly losing credibility because he had made a promise to give something that now he wouldn't or couldn't give. His clients and he had little leverage: our clients were the ones who had the money the deal required, so our clients had the leverage, and that was clear to everyone in the room. You see, a legal opinion is a written document under which a law firm gives certain assurances as to facts and legal issues, and the law firm is liable if those assurances are inaccurate—and, in this case, this lawyer was not willing to put his firm on the line. Despite the lack of leverage, the lawyer was pounding the table, acting the tough guy. It was not just a tactic—he was clearly furious, yelling, "You know nobody could give that opinion!"

Mike looked up and calmly said, "How would I know that? You said you were going to give it. Why wouldn't I believe you?"

We took a break, and the management team went to confer in one of the exterior offices. We were on the fifty-third floor of the building, and there were numerous morbid jokes about how it was a good thing that the windows didn't open. To say that the would-be buyers were distraught is putting it mildly—if this deal didn't close, they would be financially ruined.

After the break, we all filed back into the room. As a summer associate, my job was just to make copies and proofread documents—certainly not to offer negotiating input. This was my first experience in a high-stakes negotiation, and I was eagerly taking it all in.

Finally, the lawyers for the buyers stated flatly that they were not going to give in, no matter what. I glanced over at Mike to read his reaction; he just sat there, pulling sheets off of his pad, one by one, and calmly crumpling them in his hands. What was he doing? By this time, it was 1:30 a.m., and the air was simultaneously heavy with exhaustion and crackling with tension.

The buyers glanced at each other. One of them turned to their attorneys, his face lined with frustration, and said, "You're fired. You won't give us the opinion; you're killing us! You're fired!"

Mind you, this was one of the major New York City law firms, and they fired them, just like that. I had never seen anything like it—

and over thirty years later, that is still the only time I have ever seen someone fire a law firm in front of everyone during a deal negotiation.

I looked again at Mike, but Mike was still just sitting there, crumpling up page after page like it was his job—the calm center of the tornado raging around him.

The fired lawyers packed up their cases and left. Now what? The deal had been in negotiation for months, and it couldn't be closed without lawyers. Mike looked up from his paper crumpling and said, "All right, why don't we all call it a night and reconvene in the morning."

Heads down and dismayed, people started to file out. I walked out next to Mike. I looked up at him—I'm sure he could read the anxiety on my face. Then, to my amazement, he smiled. He put his arm around my shoulder and said, "Hey, don't worry about it, kid. This deal is going to close."

I was not about to argue with him, but I was thinking, *How could he know that? It seems like the thing's dead.* Still, he had said it with such clarity and with such a calm energy that it made me wonder what he knew that nobody else in the room knew. By this time, it was after two in the morning. We agreed to reconvene at 8 a.m. I would grab what sleep I could in the meanwhile, but I doubted the buyers would be getting much rest.

We all returned at 8 a.m. the next morning. Mike waited for all of us to be seated, and then the "Masterful One" divulged to the rest of us something he had known all along—the deal would close that day. Behind the scenes, sometime between 2 a.m. and 8 a.m., he had moved things forward, had the management team rehire their lawyers, and resolved all of the open issues.

It wasn't until later that I found out that Mike had seen all along that the law firm would never give the opinion, even back when they had said they would months before. He knew that ultimately, when they looked into it, they would realize that doing so would put them at too much risk and that when push came to shove, they would refuse to stick their necks out.

You see, this was a legal opinion nobody else had ever given—a major point regarding bankruptcy risk and upstream guarantees. Mike knew from day one that they would, very likely, never give that opinion, and he foresaw there would come a point at which they would have to back away from that promise. He had known that months in advance, but he just let it play out because he knew that, down the line, he would inevitably advise our client to give on that point.

He anticipated that he would then be able to get other things that the client wanted in exchange for the concession because, by that point, the buyers so desperately wanted the deal done. They were obsessing about the one issue that they thought was going to kill the deal, so once we got by that, they were happy to agree to pretty much anything.

I'm not suggesting that Mike abused this opportunity or used it to take advantage of the buyers; "Oh now they're so desperate, I'm going to crush them." It wasn't like that at all. These were issues that were important to our client and appropriate to negotiate; Mike got the concessions he needed to meet his client's objectives, and he got them faster and without additional concessions from our client. He wasn't interested in destroying or embarrassing the buyers; he just got what the client needed, and we got the deal done. What struck me most was not just that the deal went from dead to closed but also

Mike's clarity and how he had achieved the desired objectives while keeping centered and calm when everyone else was losing their cool.

Wow, how does he do that? I wondered. Having that kind of long-range vision seemed something akin to a superpower to me, newbie that I was. It reminded me of postgame interviews I'd seen with football quarterbacks, when they would describe seeing the field differently from how you or I would see it in the heat of the game. It is as though they *felt* what was going to happen and they controlled the pass and sent it exactly where it had to be, no matter what was going on around them, because they had this kind of extraordinary clarity. The first time I really saw that up close and in a negotiation was with Mike; Mike was "in the zone."

Up until then, I had assumed a powerful negotiator looked like someone who made the best arguments and outwardly showed

> **Up until then, I had assumed a powerful negotiator looked like someone who made the best arguments and outwardly showed strength.**

strength. Listen, sometimes table banging is going to be "effective"—at least in the short term. I don't think it's the best way to go though, because in many deals, we have to live together and we develop a negotiating reputation that could reduce deal opportunities. Also, no matter how desperate you may think people are, sometimes they will walk. But certainly in this scenario, where the table-banging attorney didn't have the leverage, it was not effective. It was only Mike being so adept at seeing the big picture and keeping his cool that kept the deal from blowing up. It wasn't just because he knew they would likely not give the legal opinion, although that was what caused most of the drama. He also foresaw how many other aspects of the negotiation would play out. Let's say instead that Mike had been a table banger or had reacted to the other attorney's table banging with anger or resentment; the deal might not have ever happened.

I was a logical kid, so I would always try to use logic to win people over to my way of thinking. But what I didn't realize until that morning is that the mental state of the negotiator—the level of clarity and calm in the inner state that he or she brings to the room—makes the critical difference. It's not just about who has the leverage or who can make the most logical argument, because that doesn't always carry the day.

Since Mike didn't spend much time pondering over or explaining how or why he did something, I didn't have the opportunity to ask him about his approach to negotiating or to get any formal training from him. Even if he had been inclined to explain his process to me, I don't think he could have verbalized it. Mike was—like many masters—an unconscious competent, someone who is really good at something but doesn't understand why they are and has never figured out exactly how they arrive at their success. This set me on a journey to understand what Mike probably didn't understand about his own mastery and to develop my own.

About three years later, I was working in another firm with a man who had the reputation of being a great negotiator. Bob was a partner at the firm, and I was a third-year associate hoping to learn from him. His methods, I soon saw, were the polar opposite of Mike's, just typical tough-guy postures. One of those postures was being obstinate, saying no without further discussion. There are situations in which that posture can be appropriate, but this man used it like a club. Predictably, Bob was a yeller and a table-banger, too. Short and stocky, his personality was bellicose, and even his younger partners were intimated by him.

He was one of the people who initially interviewed me for the job. His interview style was to fire questions like a machine gun, presumably in an attempt to knock you off balance. I sat there, sweating, trying to answer as quickly as I could get the words out. Some of the questions were personal, some were about my experience; he just kept them coming, barely waiting to hear the answers. We were twenty questions in, and he was still firing away—"So you went to NYU Law?"

"Yes."

"How many deals have you done?"

"Uh . . . about forty."

"Explain to me a reverse triangular merger." I did so.

Then Bob said, "You live in Forest Hills, Queens; there's an ice cream shop—"

At that point, I practically leapt from my seat, pointed at him, and shouted, "Eddie's Sweet Shop!"

He beamed at me. "That's it!"

Somehow I passed my interview by knowing that Eddie's Sweet Shop was the best ice cream shop in Forest Hills. And that's the way Bob negotiated. He was a bulldozer, and he kept coming at you. He wouldn't take no for an answer.

What I realized over time, though, was that there wasn't much to him beyond his tough-guy posturing. In situations where Bob had the leverage, most often he would be "successful," in that he would get what he needed for the client (at least in the short term). But in situations where he didn't have the leverage, he was most often unsuccessful. Even in those circumstances, he wouldn't change the way he behaved; Bob would never shift his approach, regardless of the situation. That was also instructive for me because I realized that anyone could be a tough guy—but how do you successfully negotiate when you are not representing the party that has all the leverage? In many scenarios, that is going to be the case—the person across the table from you may hold most of the cards, while you hold few, or the bargaining positions are comparable.

In fact, most often when you're doing a deal, even a less-complex deal, each side has something with which to bargain. Let's say you're trying to attract a key executive or other employee for your firm. Chances are that your candidate wouldn't have applied unless she

Anyone could be a tough guy—but how do you successfully negotiate when you are not representing the party that has all the leverage?

had interest in the job—but she might have other offers or hopes of them. And, of course, there are also always other potential candidates. If you're buying a house, even a house you're in love with, there are always other houses. These aren't usually lopsided situations. Typically, one side will have more leverage than the other, but it's not generally a dominant advantage. And even in a situation where somebody seems to have overriding leverage, the ultimate leverage point that the weaker party always has is simply walking away from the deal. You may think they won't, but you never know until they actually do it. So, in reality, nobody ever has zero cards to play; they hold, at the least, the walk-away card.

It's easy to get clients what they want when they are the ones with the leverage. To me, this is not the sign of a great negotiator; great negotiators are those who get those clients with less leverage more of what they want and who attain fair and lasting deals even when they have the leverage.

I thought back to Mike and wondered again, *How did he do that?*

It was interesting to me as a young attorney to work for these two polar-opposite negotiators: the Zen-like negotiator, Mike, who seemed totally in control of himself and of the situation in the room at all times (but who, interestingly, was far from Zen in his everyday personality), and Bob—a furious little fireplug of a guy whose whole routine was variations on strong-arming the opposition. One was coming from a place of genuine strength, the other merely doing his best to imitate it.

One was coming from a place of genuine strength, the other merely doing his best to imitate it.

I decided pretty quickly which of the two I'd rather be like.

CHAPTER TWO

CLARITY, DETACHMENT, AND EQUILIBRIUM (CDE)

The Framework for Authentic Negotiating Success

The journey that my experience with Mike started me on has led to this book. This book is the result of more than thirty years of study, analysis, practice, and, most importantly, attaining results. That thirty-plus-year journey has resulted in my philosophy and practice of Authentic Negotiating. Authentic Negotiating is a different way of looking at negotiating. It is not about the tactics and techniques that are the basis of a lot of the other material about negotiating (the worst of which are manipulative and inauthentic and the best of which may be useful but do not go to the core of what makes the most difference in negotiating success). It is about the harder work that makes the real difference in negotiating success. It's about CDE: Clarity, Detachment, and Equilibrium.

CLARITY

Most people go into negotiations without doing the work they need to do to become crystal clear on the outcomes they want to achieve, what their true bottom line is, and under what circumstances they will agree or not agree to a deal. Understanding how to obtain total Clarity is the first crucial step to becoming a great negotiator. As I will detail later in the book, this requires a level of self-knowledge, a connection to inner truth, and a willingness to delve deep that many are not willing to do the work to access.

> **Understanding how to obtain total Clarity is the first crucial step to becoming a great negotiator.**

DETACHMENT

The next key body of work is around Detachment—detaching yourself from the outcome. When you enter into a negotiation, your preference should be that you get the deal done—buy the company, close the distribution deal, sell that property, etc.—or why would you be in that negotiation? However, in the end, you need to be detached from the outcome. If you are able to achieve the objectives on which you have Clarity, then you do the deal. If not, you don't. It's that simple. No hard feelings; it's just not the deal for you. You must trust that another, better deal will come along or that this one was simply not meant to be. Great negotiators are always willing to walk away—not from a place of anger or ego but from a place of Detachment based upon their Clarity.

> Great negotiators are always willing to walk away—not from a place of anger or ego but from a place of Detachment based upon their Clarity.

EQUILIBRIUM

The third key to negotiating success is being able to maintain your Equilibrium during the entire negotiation. Staying centered, calm, and clear, without getting thrown off by the tactics, techniques, or emotions of the other side or your own emotions, is the final, crucial element.

As I discuss in the upcoming chapters, the body of work to master CDE not only has a significant external preparation component but an even more important, and often overlooked or shortchanged, body of internal work that you must do to significantly increase your chances of negotiating success. Although most would acknowledge the value of CDE, few people achieve it in their negotiations because they are not willing to do what it takes. As in many other aspects of life, it seems easier to look for the shortcut—the tip, tactic, or technique that will help you win.

Considering that we all negotiate every day, and our success or failure in negotiation has such a huge impact on our goals, desires, and dreams, I urge you to be one of the few willing to do the work necessary to master CDE. Whether you negotiate in business (as with customers, employees, vendors, businesses, partners, investors, or strategic and other deal partners) or in life (as with contractors, home buyers/sellers, neighbors, teachers, and family members), the outcomes of those negotiations will shape your future.

CHAPTER THREE

THE TOP SIX REASONS NEGOTIATIONS FAIL

t some point in your career, you've probably been on the losing side of a negotiation. Here are six of the most common reasons for negotiating failure:

1. Lack of preparation

2. Ego

3. Fear

4. Rigidity

5. Getting emotional / losing objectivity

6. Lack of integrity

LACK OF PREPARATION

EXTERNAL PREPARATION

Research, research, research—the company, market, industry, etc. I am not going to go into detail on all of the aspects of external preparation here. There are many other resources that cover this. The purpose of this section is to focus on just a couple of areas in which many people fail.

DO YOU KNOW WHO IS ON THE OTHER SIDE OF THE TABLE?

Many people will do their due diligence on the company involved, but they won't do any research on the individual negotiator or negotiators with whom they are dealing. Having insights about whoever is on the other side of that table can make or break a negotiation, and you should never neglect that effort.

That negotiator could be the business owner, it could be the salesperson, or it could be their acquisitions person or their procurement person. Knowing what this person's personal investment is in the outcome is critical, and so is knowing their individual style, preferences, motivations, and objectives. For example, your deal may be a great thing for the company, but if you can't get that individual negotiator on board, you are probably never going to get anybody else in the company to see the value of the deal. He may have his own objectives, fears, or concerns that keep him from negotiating. There may be a divisional budget he's worried about, for instance.

One of the biggest factors when you negotiate with people who work for somebody else, as opposed to negotiating directly with the business owner, is that often the number-one place they are coming from is fear of something going wrong. This is especially true in larger deals. If the people across the table from you recommended making this deal or are assigned to do a deal with you and it doesn't work out, failure can come back to bite them. Their jobs could be on the line, or their promotion or bonus at risk. Certainly, their standing and credibility could be adversely impacted. You'll want to take that into account, because if they perceive the potential for harm to themselves to be too great, you may never get past their personal issues or concerns or fears, no matter how much sense this deal makes for the company they represent.

Do as much research as you can ahead of your initial meeting. The Internet is obviously a rich mine of information on people, if you're willing to dig a little. You can also size your counterpart up once you're in the room together. If there's anything you can't gather before you meet, you want to be ready to ask the right questions in order to figure out where these people are coming from. What are their personal motivations, fears, and goals? Naturally, you're not going to ask them those questions outright, but you can ask questions that elicit that information.

Once you have a sense of what their personal investments are, you can use that knowledge to help them be comfortable that this deal is going to work to their credit.

Once you have a sense of what their personal investments are, you can use that knowledge to help them be comfortable that this deal is going to work to their credit, that nobody's going to come back to them and say, "Why the hell did you do this?" It's not going to blow up in their face; in fact, maybe it will make them look great. By knowing where they are coming from, you'll be in a better place to reassure them or help them feel comfortable.

What kinds of questions might you ask? You could ask about prior deals they have done and what worked or didn't work. You can also ask questions related to what upper management is looking for and how they can help deliver it. Depending on their personality, you can try to connect with them on a more personal level by asking about their interests, their family, or where they are from. The key is to be genuinely interested in that person's story, not just doing this as a tactic, which will come across as insincere.

HAVE YOU PREPARED AND ACCOUNTED FOR CULTURAL DIFFERENCES?

The next big issue that people often don't consider enough is cultural differences. This topic could easily fill an entire book, and given its complexity and the other resources available in this area, I'm not going to delve into it too deeply. But there are certainly significant cultural differences in negotiating styles and approaches, including the sense of what is proper and what is considered good etiquette, that negotiators too often ignore to their peril.

Whether you're negotiating internationally or domestically, in different geographic regions from which you are accustomed, intergenerationally, or in a different business culture (like financial services vs. technology or Wall Street vs. Silicon Valley), it is essential to do due diligence and research on those cultural, geographic, and generational differences.

I remember when I was a young associate at a major national law firm in the late 1980s. We had a sizeable deal to negotiate with a Japanese company, so we hired a cultural consultant to help us prepare. She told us what to do when somebody gives us a business card, for instance, an aspect of their traditions that we might easily have overlooked. How you accept a person's card in Japan is very different from how it is done in the US. With the Japanese, you don't just take a glance at the business card and stick it in your pocket; you take it with both hands and hold it in front of you, you read it, and you look at the person and acknowledge that they have given it to you. Then you put it down on the conference table in front of you. If you don't follow that protocol, it's an insult—and the last way you want to begin an important meeting is by insulting your counterparts across the table—even inadvertently. That's why I would strongly suggest preparing on that topic when you are meeting someone from a culture whose conventions are unfamiliar to you.

Now, let's move on and focus more much deeply on the part of preparation that is much less talked about and done much less frequently or fully.

INTERNAL PREPARATION

All of this pregame external research and due diligence is simply table stakes—you shouldn't be in the game without it. What should also be table stakes but is far too often skimped on or avoided and is taught much less

All of this pregame external research and due diligence is simply table stakes—you shouldn't be in the game without it.

often is the internal preparation (which is why I am going to focus on it a lot more than on external preparation).

WHAT ARE YOUR OBJECTIVES AND WHAT ABOUT YOU STANDS IN THE WAY OF ACHIEVING THEM?

First, consider the objectives. Yes, of course, look at their objectives, but what are your objectives? How do you become crystal clear on all of them? What are your true motivations, and what are the limiting beliefs, fears, or other emotions that might hold you back? Most of us don't take the time and are not willing to do the hard internal work to address these and attain the level of clarity required to be a great negotiator.

DO YOU KNOW WHAT YOUR TRUE BOTTOM LINE IS?

Define your true bottom line.

This is an exercise I always do with clients when they are preparing for an important negotiation. Few people do this exercise at the depth I insist with myself and my clients: define your true bottom line. It's very easy to look at it in terms of money—"What's the bottom line? I won't take less than x dollars." But it actually applies to every term in the negotiation, and those terms may not all be monetary: they might concern the delivery time of the product or how you'll get paid or how long you'll stay on as an employee or consultant to the new owner if you are selling or merging your company.

Your true bottom line in this last instance could involve a specific limit on how long you have to stay on, so you might say, "I'm not willing to enter into an employment contract for more than two years. That's my bottom line on the deal. Everything else could be right, but if they want me for more than two years, I won't do it." The true bottom line can apply to every single term in the deal. Of course, you're not going to waste your time establishing this for every minor point, but for the major points, it is crucial that you know what your true bottom line is.

When it comes to true bottom lines, people lie to themselves and to their advisors all the time. Sometimes even while they're not consciously lying, they're not fully connected to the truth. I've seen it play out, as the goalposts on their bottom line shift in the midst of the deal-making process. They may start out saying that, "My bottom line is *x*," but then the next thing you know, they're 20 percent below *x* as the negotiations grind on, and then the whole negotiating strategy that was designed based on the original bottom line gets compromised.

> When it comes to true bottom lines, people lie to themselves and to their advisors all the time.

How can you define your true bottom line in a meaningful way and stick to it? This is a key part of the work I do with my clients in the CDE process when we're preparing for a negotiation. Let's say Maria is selling her company. She tells me, "I'd love to get $1.5 million; realistically I hope to get $1.2 million, but I won't take anything below $1 million."

"So your bottom line is $1 million?" I ask.

"Yes, $1 million," Maria says.

"Okay, just so we're clear here. You're saying that if they offered you $999,999.99, you would walk?"

"Oh, come on. That's kind of ridiculous. It's only a penny."

"Okay. What if it's $999,999.98? $.97? $.96? My point is that it can always be a penny less. You could do that until you got to zero. So there's got to be a number that you literally will not take a penny under. If that is $1 million, then that means you do not take $999,999.99 if it's offered—you turn the deal down.

"Ah, I get it. Yes. One million—not a penny less."

"Okay, great. Now we can start to design the negotiating strategy."

Again, this applies to the nonmonetary terms, too; it's the same concept. Take the assertion, "I won't work for more than two years." Okay—but will you work for two years and a day? Two years and two days? It must be "not a day more, not a penny less." This defining exercise is tremendously useful to my clients because it brings their goals into sharp focus for them. The reason that's so crucial is because you're going to design your entire negotiating strategy around this, so you must go in with clarity about where that bottom line is. So few do that level of internal preparation or get to that level of clarity.

> **Without knowing your true bottom line on all of the material points and how they interrelate, you can never achieve clarity at the level you must have to significantly increase your chances of success in a negotiation.**

As you can see, true bottom line is a key component to the C in CDE—Clarity. Without knowing your true bottom line on all of the material points and how they interrelate, you can never achieve clarity at the level you must have to significantly increase your chances of success in a negotiation. So, in addition to determining the bottom line on each deal term, you should rank them by priority and determine how they relate to each other. If—in a vacuum—your bottom line on a post-sale employment contract is one year, are you willing to extend that period if, for example, they offer you another $500,000 in purchase price or you can negotiate a shorter payment schedule?

TRUSTING YOUR HIRED NEGOTIATORS

If somebody or a team is negotiating on another person's behalf, whether it's a lawyer, investment banker, or some other paid negotiator, sometimes their client will not give their negotiator their true bottom line, because they're afraid. This happens all the time with real estate brokers on houses. People say to the real estate broker, "My bottom line is this," when in fact they have some flexibility on price. Why? They don't trust the real estate broker not to sell them out. They're thinking, *The commission difference for my broker is not big. They'll forego a few bucks to get an easy deal done, as opposed to negotiating hard on my behalf.* That's a problem if it's true, but a more significant problem is that now the client is lying to their own broker. I'm not saying that in certain situations it may not be warranted, but there is a better way.

And that better way is even more crucial when the deal is more important. Especially in a deal of any significance, where you have a lawyer or an investment banker or other professional negotiating on your behalf, you must be fully honest for that person to properly represent you. If you don't trust somebody enough to give them your true bottom line, then you need to look for someone else to work with whom you can trust.

EGO

There are so many situations in which I've seen ego wreck a negotiator's game. Ego puts people off, comes across as inauthentic, and allows the other side to control and manipulate you. Its primary "tells" are pride, wanting to be liked, the need to win as opposed to achieving your objectives, and the need to look good, which can push you to act like a tough guy or gal because your ego tells you that your reputation is somehow on the line. If the other side says something that triggers your pride, that can swiftly derail you emotionally, creating anger, frustration, or hurt. I've seen far too many instances in which the negotiator blows the deal because of ego—literally walks out of the room or digs in and gets obstinate.

> **Ego puts people off, comes across as inauthentic, and allows the other side to control and manipulate you.**

THE PITFALLS OF PRIDE

Pride is just another way in which people can get triggered and thrown off. Here's a classic example. The founder of a company, who built his company from scratch and has been running it for twenty-five years, decides that it is time for him to sell it. He wants $10 million for the company. A potential buyer approaches him and says, "Listen, the company is not worth $10 million. It's worth $8 million because your computer systems are outdated. Your logo and marketing have to be updated. Your competitors have evolved more quickly in the new marketplace." The owner's pride is hurt. This is his baby. He built it. How does he react? With anger because his pride is wounded. "How can he tell me that it's not worth my asking price? That guy doesn't know what he's talking about!" The owner is not viewing the situation objectively.

Granted, the other side might be saying that as a tactic, but it could be accurate. In the case of a sale of a business, founders often have an inflated view of the value of their firm because they are looking at what they put into it over twenty-five years, and building it was their life. But, of course, buyers don't look at it that way. The question from their point of view is, what's the market value of the company? The value of the company has nothing to do with whether you built it in twenty-five years or five years, or worked eighty hours a week or forty hours a week—but the owner doesn't want to hear that. Any time people get triggered because their pride is hurt, it is like any other situation in which they get triggered emotionally; they're likely to veer off center, they can lose perspective, and then they're in a weakened position in terms of negotiating. Don't be one of those people.

Another way in which pride can undermine you is if your pride makes you unable to admit that you don't actually have a piece of information that you need. People who can't admit to what they don't know run themselves into trouble, because they may give a concession that they shouldn't give or refuse one that they ought to give. They're afraid that, if they admit they're unsure of something, it will make them look bad or lose credibility. Perhaps, again, they're fearful that could threaten their job. But playing

But playing your hand in ignorance can certainly undermine you and your credibility just as badly.

your hand in ignorance can certainly undermine you and your cred-ibility just as badly.

If your pride stops you from admitting that you aren't clear on a particular point, or tempts you to bluff your way through something, and the other side finds out down the line that you've misrepresented information, that could blow the deal. Then they'll say, "We can't trust this person to tell us the truth. What else about this deal might he be covering up or misrepresenting?"

WANTING TO BE LIKED

The other side of the situation, which people don't realize, is that sometimes ego can show up in a way that resembles weakness. Our ego wants us to be liked by other people. We don't want to look bad in front of others. Sometimes, to be liked, we give too many conces-sions. I had a client once who was a graphic designer who had the opportunity to design something for a music star. The designer was a huge fan. She wanted so much for this celebrity to like her that she ended up doing twice the amount of work while negotiating her fee down by half—all without a written contract—and then never got the recognition she wanted, and, on top of that, the celebrity client ended up not paying a penny of her reduced fee. When wanting to be liked is our driver, we end up with deals that are not good for us or that we are not ultimately going to be happy with or that are not close to the best

If the other side senses that need to be liked or unwillingness to stand for what you want for fear of looking bad, they can use that against you.

deal we could have gotten, because we desperately want the other people to like us. If the other side senses that need to be liked or unwillingness to stand for what you want for fear of looking bad, they can use that against you. If they, for example, try to portray you as the bad guy or gal, and psychologically that bothers you, then they have thrown you off your game.

Let's say they bring up something that you're really unsure of (for example, they want some additional services that you need to subcontract and they insist that you quote full pricing, including those subcontracted services, on the spot). You don't know the answer they're asking for—you don't have the full information you need to properly determine the price in my example, and you don't know how to handle it in the moment. As opposed to being confident and strong enough in yourself to say, "I don't know right now. Why don't we hold off on that point and let me get back to you with the full pricing? We can discuss that next time," or, "Let me step out of the room. I need to check this with somebody," or, "I need more time to think about that," you get nervous because the ego is telling you, "You're going to look bad here, you don't want them to think you're stupid." Because you are feeling insecure, you agree to go along with something that is against your interests. You quote that price without the information you need to be sure it is right.

We're all human, but any time you feel your pride pushing itself to the forefront, or sense that you're feeling the need to look good, to be liked, or to not seem stupid or unprepared, it should be a signal to you that you must beware. You may not be in the best emotional position to successfully negotiate, and you have to do something to try to get recentered—to reestablish your Equilibrium.

The CDE framework, the CPR tool I discuss in chapters 6 and 7, and the other advice in this book are all intended to support you in staying out of your ego. Remember: it's not about you; it is about achieving your objectives. A negotiation is not the place to work out your issues over being rejected or about anger or hurt from your past. If you want to substantially increase your negotiating success, do the internal work to let go of your ego and the past issues that trigger it, or at least be able to put them aside for the purposes of the negotiation. This one point is more valuable than any tactic or countertactic you will ever learn.

ARE YOU LOOKING TO ACHIEVE YOUR OBJECTIVE OR JUST TO WIN?

My goal is *never* to win a negotiation.

Yes, you read that right—my goal is *never* to win a negotiation. My goal is always to achieve my or my client's objectives.

In a way, that could seem like a subtle distinction because if I achieve the objectives, haven't I won? Well, yes, you could say it's a way we define what winning means. But very often, in the heat of the moment, people lose track of what they are really trying to achieve.

> My goal is *never* to win a negotiation. My goal is always to achieve my or my client's objectives.

Some people get into the negotiations room and get caught up in the tension of the back and forth. They need to walk out of there feeling like they've won that round. Sometimes it's better to lose a round in a negotiation if that's what it takes to get you to your ultimate objectives. That need to win is triggered by the ego. If you determine that you have somebody on the other side of the table that has a high need to win, you can use that to allow them to win, while still achieving all of your objectives—but you can only do that if you don't let your own ego get in your way.

For those people who must win, for example, you might be slower to concede on issues that you know you would ultimately have given in on anyway, because you've determined that this other person must feel like they've battled and won. If you give in too easily, they're going to find another issue to battle you on. So you hold out on certain points longer, even though you're going to concede them. That way, you can let them feel like they've won; meanwhile, you've traded that off for other points you really do care about. I have said that tactics aren't all bad. This is one that works when you've taken the deeper look and realized, *This person is in a place of ego. This is the kind of person who needs to win.* You, however, are clear on your objectives and not going to get thrown off by the bullying your opponent may be exhibiting, because you know where they're coming from, and you don't need to win. You have Clarity, you are Detached from the outcome, and you maintain your Equilibrium. Remember, there is always more than one path to reaching your objectives. When you have Clarity and maintain your Equilibrium, you are much more likely to be able to see the alternative routes.

A good illustration of that is an interesting deal that I did in the 1990s in the early days after the end of the Cold War. Business was just starting to open up in Russia, but the Russian businesspeople there had no cash. Their access to foreign currency was limited, and they couldn't get money out of the country, so they were trying to do everything by barter. I had a client who was approached by a group out of Russia that, surprisingly, had money and had it in the US. The Russian group had done a deal with Perdue to purchase enough chicken to fill half of a huge tanker ship, which had nothing to do with our part of the deal. My client, Jeffrey, was contracted to fill the other half of this tanker ship with tons and tons of other goods. His job for this Russian group was to source the goods, which were the stereotypical sorts of merchandise you'd have expected to be in demand back then—blue jeans, cigarettes, and electronics, everything that they wanted in Russia during those days that wasn't easy to get.

We had some very tough negotiations with these guys. One sticking point was an issue that was standard in agreements of this kind in the US—what we call a non-circumvention clause—but the Russians weren't willing to do it, and it could easily have blown the whole deal. Jeffrey was the middleman; he introduced the Russians to manufacturers and distributors who would provide their group with the goods they wanted. My client, as was typical, was to be paid a commission for doing that. What is standard in those agreements is for the buyer to agree, "If I introduce you to XYZ Company, and you subsequently do the deal for blue jeans or televisions or whatever, you're not going to go directly to them and cut me out of the deal now or in the future." The Russian team flatly refused to agree to that, which left us wondering, "How can we possibly do a deal?"

Here's where the example applies about keeping your eye on objectives and not on needing to win on a particular negotiating point made all the difference. With our help, Jeffrey had laid out a list of objectives that included the amount of money he wanted to make in sourcing all the goods they wanted, along with other key terms. One of the things on the list was certainly to have protection from them cutting him out of that deal and future deals. When we hit this sticking point over the non-circumvention clause, it started to get very heated in the negotiation room, and I said, "Let's take a break." We didn't have a lot of time to get this done, but I knew that if we couldn't solve this issue, the deal was dead.

I took my client outside, and I said, "Jeff, listen, just relax. Let's table that issue."

He said, "Why would we table that issue? That's a deal-breaker."

I said, "Because I think I have an alternative solution. So just trust me, and let's put that aside and see if we can get the other issues resolved." He trusted me, so he agreed.

When we went back into the room. I said to their lead negotiator, "Listen, Evgeny, it's evident that this is a highly contested issue. Why don't we just leave it alone for now? We'll come back to it maybe the next time we sit down. Let's talk about what else we have open." And we did. After the fact, I said to my client, "Here's the deal. Think about it; do we care whether or not they agree to a non-circumvention clause?"

"Of course we care, Corey. I wouldn't do the deal without it."

I said, "No, hang on Jeff, listen to what I'm saying. Do we care that they agree to this clause?"

He still didn't see where I was going. I continued, "What we care about is that we get that protection that they can't go around you. That is our objective. We don't care how we get it. We just care that we get it."

"I guess you're right. But what are you proposing?"

"Think about it. We're doing a deal with a group out of Russia. Yeah, they set up a US company, but we don't really know how credible or liquid they are. We have no ability to do any real due diligence on them, which is why we're getting our cash up front. How are we going to enforce this non-circumvention clause, even if they did agree to it? How useful is it? Let me ask you something. You have good relationships with all of the suppliers and manufacturers who are supplying the goods, right?"

"Yeah."

"So I know that it is more typical to get the non-circumvent from the buyer, but let's go get the agreement from your suppliers and manufacturers. They won't do any additional business with the Russian group unless we get paid, right? They're US companies. We know where to find them." Honestly, it was a better way to secure that objective than trying to win the argument with the Russians.

Jeffrey thought that was brilliant, but again it was really a matter of keeping our eye on achieving our objectives as opposed to winning that negotiating point. We could in fact achieve the objective without winning that argument. It was a question of finding another way to do it.

> **We could in fact achieve the objective without winning that argument.**

There were a few days between that session and the next negotiating session. During that downtime, we locked up agreements with all of the suppliers and manufacturers who agreed not to do any subsequent business with the Russians without going through my client—mission accomplished. That way, when we went back into the negotiating room, we were able to trade off what seemed like a huge concession; we said we would give in on that big issue about them signing a non-circumvention in exchange for three other things we wanted. Thus, we ended up apparently capitulating on an issue that actually didn't matter to us anymore. So they "won," but we achieved our objective and got them to agree to three other things without any loss on our side.

The key to that success was focusing on our objectives, not letting our egos engage, and thus, releasing any need to win a point on which the Russians seemed to be taking an irrational position. It also required us to be flexible on how we got there and not to insist on being "right." Here is an interesting question to look at. Why was the Russian side so adamant about this one thing? To understand their position, it's important to remember that this was shortly after the fall of communism. What they said was, "We're now capitalists. We're businesspeople. We've gone our entire lives with the Soviet government telling us who we could or could not do business with. That time is over. We will not be restricted in who we can do business with." No matter how absurd that seems to us, they were serious about it. It would have been easy to be reactive and say, "That's stupid. That's crazy. What are you guys doing?" But instead, we stepped back, recognized that there was a cultural context for their position, heard where they were coming from, and found another solution.

THE DANGERS OF TALKING TOO MUCH

Talking too much can also be a tell for people who are very ego-driven. Sometimes it comes from simply liking to hear themselves talk. These people think they are smarter than everybody in the room. The more you talk, however, the more information you are giving away, especially to a good negotiator. When someone is talking, I sit there reading them, paying close attention not only to what they say but also to the tonality of their voice, to their facial expressions, and to their body language. They're effectively handing me information that is only going to help me. If I'm smart, I'm going to sit there quietly, letting the person bloviate, and take it all in.

> The more you talk, however, the more information you are giving away, especially to a good negotiator.

The other thing about people who talk too much out of ego is that they usually are correspondingly not good listeners. The other side will start talking, and they will barely listen because they're already formulating their next brilliant remark. It's certainly easier to fall into that in a negotiation where the paradigm is traditionally back and forth: "I want this. You want that. I'll give you this. You give me that. Here is why you're wrong. Here is why I'm right." It's set up in a way that means you're always thinking ahead to your next point. But the problem is that if that causes you not to pay attention to the other side—not only not listening to them, but not watching them, either—then you are missing the opportunity to gather phenomenal information that could give you an advantage in the negotiation.

Talking too much out of ego also takes away the power of silence. It's amazing how many people don't use silence effectively. In the case of the ego-driven talker, it's because they need to hear themselves talk. But silence gives you a lot. Most people are uncomfortable in silence, but if you are willing and able to be silent, it is a great negotiating tool. If your silence comes from a place of CDE, as opposed to being a game, then you truly have a huge advantage.

> **Most people are uncomfortable in silence, but if you are willing and able to be silent, it is a great negotiating tool.**

For instance, if you say, "Listen, we need eight weeks for delivery on that. That's the best we can do, eight weeks for delivery on that product," and the other side doesn't respond right away, what might be your response to their lack of response? If you know you can actually deliver in six weeks but you want that cushion, often you'll be tempted to break the silence by offering that concession before it's even asked for. "You know, I said eight weeks, but we might be able to do it in seven." You're giving things away because you can't deal with the silence. That's the power of silence, particularly if the person on the other side of the table isn't comfortable with it.

FEAR

There are many ways that fear sabotages successful negotiating.

NERVES CAN MAKE YOU TALK TOO MUCH

If people are afraid, if they're uncomfortable, if they're feeling outmatched or insufficiently experienced, then the kinds of fears and the nerves they engender can betray them into talking more than they ought to. They may not have that egotistic, blowhard, "I know everything" personality; they may actually be on the opposite end of the spectrum. You see this in job interviews when somebody's nervous and they babble. It happens in negotiations, too, where somebody is feeling outmatched, feeling afraid, or feeling desperate, whether it's because they feel like they need the deal or they don't know what they're doing, and it can cause them to talk a lot.

It's a bad idea to let your tongue run away with you because inevitably you're giving away too much information, you're not listening, and you're not using the power of silence. The end result is the same as talking too much due to ego, although it comes from a different place.

How should you prepare yourself if you're aware that this is a problem? If you tend to talk a lot in the negotiations or in other pressure situations, then one of the things to determine is whether that comes out of fear or out of ego, because depending on which it is, you have to attack the issue in different ways.

FEAR OF LOSING

People's fears show up in many other ways—for some people, fear is caused by loss or the thought of losing. Really, though, this is just the other side of needing to win. Remember, negotiation is not about losing (or winning). It is about achieving your objectives. If you are afraid of losing, you have not done enough work to attain and maintain Detachment. Recognize that fear as an indicator that this is an area of CDE that you need to work on.

FEAR OF FAILURE—AND OF SUCCESS

Fear of failure is a real problem in negotiation. If I have someone on the other side of the table who is afraid that she's going to fail at the negotiation or that the deal is going to fail and she's not going to get it done, then that's going to show through in some of the ways we've previously discussed. That puts her in a weaker position.

But a less-talked-about problem is fear of success; odd as it may seem, there are people who are afraid of succeeding. I've seen it in situations, for example, where somebody has grown up with modest means and has been taught perhaps that the rich are evil people who've taken advantage of poorer people to get where they are. The associated belief is that somehow having money makes you change into someone evil. Now this person has an opportunity to do a deal that can be very lucrative and life changing for them, whether it's entering into a strategic alliance or a joint venture, negotiating a huge multiyear consulting agreement, selling her company, or making a distribution deal with a major company. That internal tension she feels, caught between the desire to do well and the fear of doing well, could derail that deal.

Often, the person who is made anxious by this fear is unaware of where it's coming from, but she reacts viscerally to those identifications with people who are wealthy because that doesn't fit her self-image. Of course, objectively, we all know it's not true that all people with money are bad or that having money will make you bad. But I've seen people sabotage their success in life and certainly in negotiations because they're afraid of exactly what they say they are trying to achieve.

If you have this issue and you don't address it, then the odds of a deal getting done are slim. As you get toward the finish line, you're going to find a reason why the deal is not going to work for you, because you're afraid of what success will do to you.

The solution? Do the deep work you need to do to identify your limiting beliefs and what might sabotage you in the negotiation. Then, when you feel the fear of success coming up (which might show up as resistance or judgment), take a step back and reconnect to why you are doing this; do your CDE preparation, and use the CPR tool that I discuss in chapters 6 and 7 to keep yourself grounded, to reconnect to your context and purpose, and then to get back in there and close that deal!

FEAR OF THE UNKNOWN

Some people fear the unknown. These are the people who will ask a million questions when you are in a negotiation with them. They can't see what the future holds, so they are determined to mine every possible bit of information from you. If you're on the other side of that, it can be annoying. You have an objective, and they're slowing the process. Their questions may seem pointless or even stupid. But if they're somebody who really needs to get comfortable, it may make sense to give them what they need. Their fears can throw a monkey wrench into the deal and potentially even stop them from following through because they're never going to get comfortable enough to sign off. I've seen this many times. Bottom line is, they're not willing to take that leap into the unknown, and there's always an unknown. Maybe that's you.

If you're merging your company, how is it going to work going forward? If you're bringing in a partner, will it work out? If you are brokering a deal, will they try to cut you out after you make the introduction? If you're buying a product, will the product meet your needs? It's easy to get waylaid by fear of the unknown.

To prevent that from happening to you, start by getting clear on what criteria you need for things to be in place after the deal. List them out. If you do the preparatory work needed to get clear with yourself and identify what really matters, then you can make sure that those points are satisfactorily addressed. This is the C in CDE—Clarity. What happens with people who are unreasonably afraid of the unknown is they often don't take the time to drill down to what they're most concerned with, which leaves them afloat in a shifting, amorphous landscape of confusion. A person in this position may not even know what it would take to satisfy that fear. In that case, it's very difficult for the other side to figure it out.

What happens with people who are unreasonably afraid of the unknown is they often don't take the time to drill down to what they're most concerned with, which leaves them afloat in a shifting, amorphous landscape of confusion.

Say, for instance, you're selling your business, but you're concerned that the buyer won't be sufficiently respectful of the client relationships you've worked to build over the years. If you're clear on that concern, you can simply say, "I need to know that my clients are going to be well taken care of, so I need to know who is going to take over these client relationships; I want to meet them and make sure I am comfortable with them." But if you have not done the work to distinguish exactly what your fear is—to get Clarity on it—then you will not know what action to take to get you comfortable enough to move forward. This is the internal work that is too often overlooked by negotiators and by those who train people to negotiate based only upon tactics and techniques.

My most recent experience of many in this area was with Fred. He was in the midst of negotiating a contract with a subcontractor who he needed for a significant contract he had won with a large municipality. The contract was the largest in his company's history by far, and this was a new subcontracting relationship, as his prior subcontractors were too small to handle the size of the job. Fred was worried about his company's ability to handle the new contract and the impact of failing to do so.

My conversation with Fred started like this:

"Corey, I don't know this subcontractor. What if they don't perform? What if they sabotage my relationship with the client? What if they don't meet the deadlines?"

"Fred, they come well recommended, right?" I verified.

"Yes."

"You told me that you did your due diligence on them and checked references and they have an excellent track record on these types of large projects."

"Yeah, but I'm just uncomfortable. You know, I've never dealt with them . . . so who knows. Also, my core team is already stretched so thin, I don't know how much harder I can work, my wife is already pissed at me because I am never home, I have my son's graduation, and we are supposed to be taking a family vacation. It's just that . . . I feel like we have no room for error, and so much can go wrong." Fred was rambling on and drowning in his uncertainty.

I said, "Fred, stop. Let's breathe and take a step back. My first question, in light of all of your concerns, is do you still want this contract or not?"

"I definitely want it. It is a game changer for my company and, ultimately, my family. Fred Jr. is starting college, and I have the two younger one's behind him, and I want them to be able to go to the best school they can get into."

I knew that taking Fred through the CDE process and having him prepare a CPR would make a huge difference for him. It did eventually, but first I needed him to surface from the ocean of fear and uncertainty that surrounded him.

"Fred, here is what I want you to do after we get off the phone. First, make a list of all of the benefits of taking and doing a great job on this contract to you, to your business, and to your family. Write them down in as much detail as you can. Then write down what additional opportunities will be available if you are wildly successful on the project. Okay?"

"Okay."

"Then brainstorm and journal about everything that you can think of that can go wrong with this project, including with the subcontractor. Then detail how you would handle each of those potential problem scenarios. What backup resources do you need to have in place? What steps can you take in advance to reduce the risk of each of these scenarios happening? What assurances do you need from the subcontractor, and what are some of the contractual protections we can add to the agreement that would make you more comfortable? Then, and this one may seem strange, envision and write down what the worst-case scenario would be if, despite all of this preparation, this project is an abject failure."

To Fred's credit, he took the coaching and did all of the homework I gave him. Four days later, I had another call with Fred. His first words were, "Corey, I'm good. Let's move forward on the subcontract."

The most interesting thing was that, out of all the homework I gave him, all of which he found useful, the most powerful part for him was envisioning and writing down the worst-case abject-failure scenarios. "It was really weird, Corey. I thought you were crazy telling me to focus on that, but when I did and I could see the worst case— even though it was bad—I knew I would be able to deal with it."

You see, Fred was not afraid of failure. He was afraid of the unknown. Once he envisioned it and wrote it down, it became known and, even though it wasn't a pretty picture, he was no longer afraid of it.

FEAR OF LOOKING BAD OR LETTING SOMEONE DOWN

Another fear that can derail your success in negotiation is the desire to not look bad. That can surface in lying about something, pumping up something, or giving into something you ought not to because you don't want to look less than informed or out of control. This is similar to the ego wanting to be liked, but for some people it shows up as fear (which often the ego tries to cover up). It comes down to not having the confidence to take a position that someone else may not like or not wanting the other person to see you as ignorant in some area.

Many people also fear letting someone down, usually somebody who is not in the room. That could be anyone from a boss or a partner, or a father or mother. This can spring from what seems to be an honorable motive. I've seen entrepreneurs, for example, who did not want to let their employees down. But if it's coming from a place of fear about what your employees will think of you, rather than from a moral commitment to do right by them, then it's not useful and can be very harmful.

> If it's coming from a place of fear about what your employees will think of you, rather than from a moral commitment to do right by them, then it's not useful and can be very harmful.

It can also be a fear of letting down family members. A classic one is the second-generation syndrome, where somebody is living out his life trying to please a parent, often a father figure. That dynamic plays into emotions that are both unhealthy and unprofitable to take into a negotiation with you. If that's a real worry for you going in, then you need to do the advance work to rid yourself of that load. In the getting Clarity process, make sure that you get to your objectives, not those of someone you are trying to avoid letting down or any other external influence, expectation, or paradigm.

RIGIDITY

Some people come in with a very rigid view of what they want in a negotiation. You already know that I preach knowing your true bottom line and getting clear on when you'll walk away. I suppose you could see that as a type of rigidity, but I'd submit that it's just Clarity and Detachment. The difference is that rigidity often shows up around how things need to look or how things need to be structured, rather than the bottom line.

PRECONCEIVED NOTIONS

Clients are funny sometimes. Miguel, a long-term client, came in once and said, "Corey, I've got a buyer for my company. I want to sell it, and I want to do it as a reverse triangular merger" (which means that the buyer creates a subsidiary company and then merges it into the company they are acquiring).

I said to him, "Okay, Miguel, I've done reverse triangle mergers. No problem if that is the way we end up going, but why do you want to structure it that way?"

"My friend did his deal as a reverse triangular merger; it worked out really well, and he saved a bunch of taxes."

I said, "That's great for him—but his deal is not necessarily your deal. Why don't we talk about where you are now, and then let's talk about your objectives and where you want to be by the end of the deal. What you pay me for is to get you there in the best way possible, and it may or may not be a reverse triangular merger." Miguel was great about it, even though he'd come in with this preconceived idea of what he wanted. Not surprisingly, his deal ended up not being structured as a reverse triangular merger, but the deal did achieve his objectives.

THE DANGERS OF INFLEXIBILITY

Some people, however, come in with preconceived notions of how things have to be—whether that's a specific type of deal structure, the purchase price, or deal terms—and insist on sticking to them, even when they're clearly not in their best interests. If you come to the negotiating process from a very rigid place, whether it's related to any particular deal point or deal structure or way things have to look, then you're teeing yourself up for failure. Yes, you need Clarity about your final destination—but a different route than the one you've set your mind on may be a quicker, smarter (or only possible) way to get there.

> If you come to the negotiating process from a very rigid place, whether it's related to any particular deal point or deal structure or way things have to look, then you're teeing yourself up for failure.

Let's be specific in drawing the distinction between Clarity and Detachment on the one hand, and rigidity on the other. Clarity and Detachment come from a centered, grounded, and connected space. There's no emotion around it; there's no tension around Clarity and Detachment. The deal works for you at x, it doesn't work for you at y. On the other hand, rigidity usually shows up with tension and emotion involved, and with reactionary energy and your ego engaged, which create the kind of inflexibility that can kill a good deal.

PACE AND TIMING

Rigidity can also reveal itself around pace and timing, and that can be a deal killer as well. Every negotiation, every deal, has its own pace and its own rhythm. On the one hand, if you slow the rhythm down too much, it adversely impacts the negotiation. People can lose interest, have more time to get worried, or come up with objections or find simpler alternatives. An equally dangerous thing is pushing the pace too fast; deals need to flow in their organic rhythm, which could be very fast, very slow, or somewhere in between, depending on the deal. Pushing a deal too hard and fast can indicate desperation, impatience, and lack of understanding or empathy, and that can cause alarm or distrust in the other party.

> **Rigidity can also reveal itself around pace and timing, and that can be a deal killer as well.**

Several years ago I had a client, Kim, who was so anxious to get out of a business partnership that she couldn't sleep at night. There was good reason to want to be out of the partnership but, unfortunately for Kim, her partner was in much less of a rush to end the relationship and was often unresponsive or significantly delayed at every step of the negotiation. The emotional toll on Kim was so great that she called me every day for updates and was even getting frustrated with me at times because I told her that pushing too hard would be counterproductive to her objectives. It was only after several long sessions with Kim in which I helped her get clear on her objectives and the best routes to achieve them and several reminders to her thereafter when her emotions triggered panic and anxiety that she was willing to surrender the pace of the negotiation that offered the best chance for a positive result—which we eventually achieved for her.

If you have a rigid view of how long things need to take, and that view isn't dictated by some very real and practical points but is arbitrary—that's rigidity. When you're rigid about a timetable without any real practical reason for it, you lose creativity. There's no time for thinking out of the box. There's no room for innovation. There's less chance of finding an alternate route when you hit a roadblock.

This kind of thinking often comes from a deep-seated fear of losing control. Whether it comes from fear or arrogance or any other driving force, it's a good way to derail a deal.

GETTING EMOTIONAL / LOSING OBJECTIVITY

There are so many situations in which our emotions can push us away from our ability to look at things objectively—our ability to maintain Equilibrium. Sometimes, it comes from being triggered in the actual negotiation by something somebody says or does or simply from the other person's approach or manipulative tactics.

And, frankly, there are simply some people whose personalities are highly emotional and reactive.

BEING CONTROLLED BY YOUR EMOTIONS IS NEGOTIATION DEATH

Whether emotion shows up as anger or as upset or as frustration—I could go on and on because this can manifest as nearly any kind of emotion—it will not serve you. Now, I'm not saying that you should be an unemotional robot, but any emotion that arises puts you at risk of losing your Equilibrium as well as your connection to the Clarity that you need. If you're really in that clear, calm place and you're Detached to the outcome—that is, you'll do the deal if it works and you won't do the deal if it doesn't—then what is there to get angry, upset, or frustrated about? Even if the other person on the other side is a jerk, reacting to that hurts you. If your counterpart is a jerk or upset, or if they're trying to trigger an emotion in you, refusal to be triggered by that gives you a tremendous advantage. It throws them off. If they do something they hope is going to upset you and you don't take the bait, then their manipulative strategy is not going to work.

> Whether emotion shows up as anger or as upset or as frustration—I could go on and on because this can manifest as nearly any kind of emotion—it will not serve you.

Sometimes people inadvertently say something that could trigger a reaction on the other side, when they didn't really mean it in the way the other person took it. If somebody says something that you think is over the line, rather than getting upset about it, isn't it better to ask clarifying questions? "Well, did you mean—?" "Why is that so important?" "Do you really believe that's true?" "Tell me more about why you think that?" If their remark has caused you to lose your Equilibrium, then you might regain it through properly understanding what the other person meant to say. If they clarify in a way that is acceptable, then you can move forward. If not, being Detached, you can make a decision from a place of Clarity on whether or not to move forward.

Especially in the midst of a negotiating session, getting emotional never helps. A lot of people make it personal, which is one of the reasons they get triggered too easily. If somebody says bluntly, "Your company's not worth that," it appears as a personal affront, as opposed to a business negotiation over terms. It's hard to step back from the emotions that statement might trigger, but you have to be able to do so because chances are that the other person meant it as a simple statement of the facts as they see them or as a negotiating tactic to drive down your price. Regardless of that person's intent, even if they meant to be offensive, getting upset about it will put you off your game.

> **Falling in love with a deal can also be a problem because it can push you into making concessions you ought not to make.**

FALLING IN LOVE WITH A DEAL

Falling in love with a deal can also be a problem because it can push you into making concessions you ought not to make. What can happen is that at the end of the negotiation you've made so many concessions that, had the deal been offered to you in those terms at the beginning, you would never have agreed to it. But it's the "death by a thousand cuts" effect; you keep saying yes because you're too much in love with the deal to say no. You agree to overlook things, or you bury issues that you should have examined more objectively.

Sometimes this happens because you have let yourself get so invested—in terms of time, money, and energy expended in making the deal work. Or you have become emotionally attached to a particular happy outcome: the sale of your business that will mean a fat check, the distribution deal you need, that big order. You start envisioning it. You start seeing it. You start tasting it. Great negotiators never fall in love with a deal. It kills Detachment.

FRUSTRATION CAN PUSH YOU IN THE WRONG DIRECTION

One of the most common ways frustration plays out is when the process isn't moving fast enough to suit you as discussed in the Rigidity section. Your response may be to start pushing the timing, sometimes to the extent that the other person or side is not comfortable and they get put off.

Alternately, you may feel that the other side is being unreasonably obstinate in not agreeing to certain points that you need, so you get frustrated and throw up your hands, as opposed to continuing to look at new ways to approach your opposition or to simply and calmly hold firm. They didn't agree to three big points you wanted? Well, why get frustrated? It's where they are. You'll either get there or you won't, and if you're not overly attached to the deal, if you can accept that it won't get done on terms that are acceptable to you, then you can let it go, because it's not meant to be and there will be another deal.

Frustration closes down your creativity and thinking. It's a form of self-sabotage and can come from emotional attachments you're not even fully aware of, but feeling the frustration is your signal to take a deeper look.

LACK OF INTEGRITY

Using any kind of dishonest tactics, including some of those old-school manipulative negotiating techniques that are taught, shows a lack of integrity. If you are manipulating somebody and not operating from a place of integrity, it's going to come back to haunt you. Of course, in a negotiation, you don't need to disclose everything that you know about your situation to the other side, but being disingenuous in any way is not the way to go, and not just because you're liable to be caught lying. First of all, a good negotiator gets a sense when you're being disingenuous. She may not know exactly what's going on, but she will sense that something's off, and that could put off a negotiation. Is it worth risking your credibility and reputation? If you're wavering, take a moment to consider just how much you're worth without those things.

When I talk about integrity and its importance in negotiations, the first thing people think of is being honest with others. Obviously, if anybody finds out that you haven't been honest with him or her, it kills your credibility. It makes him or her distrust everything else you've said.

Another form of lack of integrity, though, is not being honest with yourself.

Another form of lack of integrity, though, is not being honest with yourself. This form of lack of integrity is much less often examined. Deep down, you don't want to do a particular deal, but still you're moving forward because of pressure from family members or others or because it's what you think you should do. People often think of integrity as something that springs from some learned external code of ethics or religion. I'm a believer that truth comes from within and that if you're genuinely connected to your heart/soul and to that clear place within you, then you'll find that truth lies there. I think we move away from that as we become older and more cynical and as all the world's pressures, messages, and temptations are thrust upon us. Children don't think in terms of taking advantage of others or of being dishonest to gain advantage, and they aren't disconnected from their inner truth until they are taught to be; they're just true to who they are. People who are not aligned with their inner truth as to what they really want in a negotiation will often self-sabotage a deal because they lack the Clarity piece of CDE.

When you're out of integrity with yourself, the other side is likely to sense that by the energy you give off when you're experiencing that kind of conflict, which can make them uncomfortable as well. In a negotiation, you always have to engage and then hold to those internal values, that moral compass, because if you don't then you're not going to feel right, and it's going to negatively impact the whole interaction or lead you astray. While I could give many examples of this, the common indicator—in hindsight—is that almost always my client (or I) ignored or let logic or some other factor override a gut feeling or other internal signal that came up during the negotiating process. On the other hand, when you are in integrity with yourself, the other side senses your alignment and becomes less likely to challenge or question your resolve and more likely to become more authentic themselves.

AVOID THE TOP SIX AND BE MORE SUCCESSFUL

You'll notice what I *haven't* said is that negotiations fail because the person conducting the negotiation isn't sufficiently trained in techniques. Many people fail at negotiating because they're not willing to take the inner journey, to deal with what they have to in order to reach that level of clarity and confidence needed to go into the room without conflicted emotions, without being rigid or letting their ego take over.

Who's showing up for this negotiation? Is it you, the calm, confident, clear negotiator, or is it fearful, unconfident you? Are you mired in some sort of arrogance or ego? Are you prepared or not prepared? Before you jump to, "How am I going to approach this?" look inside yourself and figure out who's showing up. If it's the fearful, unprepared person who comes from a place of scarcity, then whatever strategy, tactics, or techniques you try are not going to work. Who you are in the negotiation is the foundation of the negotiation. If you are willing to do the work necessary to achieve Clarity, Detachment, and Equilibrium and avoid these top six reasons for negotiation failure, then your chances of negotiating success increase exponentially.

CHAPTER FOUR

THE FIVE STEPS TO BEING A GREAT NEGOTIATOR

1. *Create and stay connected to a powerful context.*

2. *Be willing to do what it takes to get to your truth.*

3. *Identify and fully own your value.*

4. *Always be in integrity.*

5. *Have high expectations.*

Before we jump into the five steps, let me discuss the state of being that underlies all of these. Great negotiating, like great leadership, is a state of being, not a skill, and it's important to understand the distinction between the two. Most courses teach negotiation as a skill, as a set of techniques, tactics, and frameworks—there is an element of those things involved, but there is much more to it. It's like the difference between having a position of leadership and being a true leader. You may have authority, but you're not necessarily a leader, because a leader leads. A leader has people who are willing to follow him or her not based upon authority but instead based upon their ability to inspire and enroll others in their vision and purpose; if you're just giving people orders, you are not actually leading them. Position doesn't make leadership. What makes leadership is the person: who he or she is and what I call his or her "state of being."

Great negotiating, like great leadership, is a state of being, not a skill.

It's the same thing in negotiating. What we're really talking about here is who you are when you come into that negotiating room—who you are being. If you are being a person who is clear, calm, collected, who doesn't let your emotions adversely impact you, and if you're detached from the outcome, then you will be more successful. If you have all kinds of styles, techniques, and tactics ready to go, but your state of being is in fear, scarcity, upset, anger, rigidity—whatever it is—then you are not going to be successful, no matter how many techniques you learn.

Instead of working so hard on tactics and techniques, *first* study the deeper qualities of successful negotiators and what they have in common: qualities like authenticity and quiet confidence. Remember Mike from chapter 1? When he walked out of that room and said, "Hey, don't worry about it, kid. This deal is going to close," I could see he had that quiet assurance, that clarity. That's why that deal got done, not because he used some technique to get it done. Who he was *being* was his ultimate technique. As I've said earlier, I don't want to say that all techniques and tactics are useless and manipulative. If you've done all the internal work and have a good handle on CDE, studying nonmanipulative techniques and tactics will make you even more powerful. Once you incorporate those deeper qualities into who you are, then you may be able to use the tactics and techniques that have integrity because now you're putting them on top of a solid base. They're like a toolbox; you can add some tools to the toolbox, but if the toolbox has holes in it and all the tools are going to fall out, adding them isn't going to do you any good.

> **Once you incorporate those deeper qualities into who you are, then you may be able to use the tactics and techniques that have integrity because now you're putting them on top of a solid base.**

I remember an attorney, Henry, who was representing clients on the other side of an unhappy split of a business partnership between three men; I represented one of the three partners, and he represented the other two. Henry called me up, yelling and screaming and threatening my client with all sorts of dire consequences. My client happened to be a lawyer, although the business he was in with the other two was not related to the law. This bullying attorney was saying, "He's going to lose his law license," and "He's unethical," neither of which was true. Henry was emotionally involved.

I'm always amazed when lawyers or other negotiators for other people get emotionally involved—and it happens more often than you'd think. It's bad enough when the client is getting emotional, but as the attorney or negotiation professional, you are the one who is being paid to be objective. You can and should be a zealous advocate for your client, but you must be able to do that without becoming emotionally triggered.

The natural reaction when somebody is coming at you is to want to go back at him, especially when he's wrong, and I remember that desire to shout back at Henry welling up in me. I wanted to tell him why he was wrong and how nothing he was saying was true, especially because my client was also a friend of mine. But I let him rant, and I kept listening to him. I didn't say a word: let him go, let him go, let him go. And eventually he ran out of steam.

Then, instead of reacting to anything he had said, I said to him, "Hey, Henry, let me ask you a question. You're representing a client. I'm representing a client. Before we get into any of the substance, why are you so worked up about this? Why are you so upset?"

He went into another long tirade about how bad and wrong my client was and why he and his clients were right. I waited for him to finish and then calmly said, "Okay, I still don't understand why you are so worked up. The way I approach things is that you and I are colleagues. We both have a job to do. There is no reason that we need to be disrespectful to each other." I didn't lecture Henry, I simply said it in a way that was true to me and as though I really didn't understand (which was true) why he was so emotionally invested in this. My response was clearly not what he'd expected, and that just totally threw him off because clearly he was used to coming at people and having them battle back. In a nice but firm way, I had called him on his approach and on his integrity. What happened? He apologized to me.

He said, "I know I can get that way sometimes. I'm just passionate about my clients."

I said, "I appreciate that, Henry. But passion, first of all, can blind you. You're not going to serve your client if you can't see clearly. I don't deal with people who are disrespectful, and if that's the way you're going to deal with me, then we don't need to talk. If you wanted to be in a lawsuit, you would have filed a lawsuit. So you're calling me to try to get a resolution without litigation. If you want to get that result with me, let's have a respectful conversation." I was very calm the whole time. I didn't get triggered by him. I knew my client's position. I practiced CDE.

Then we were able to have a discussion. Interestingly, after that discussion, he never contacted me again. I tried to follow up with him, but he never responded. It was almost as if he tried what he knew to get a result, and I didn't react in the way he expected, so it failed. I don't know if he didn't know what to do, or if he'd promised his clients a certain result and then didn't get it. To this day, I don't know what happened. We followed up later, and Henry's clients had hired another attorney.

You see, I really do practice what I preach . . . most of the time. It's become much more natural for me to stay in that calm and centered place, not getting triggered, and staying detached—that state of being I call CDE. When you do that, you don't give energy to any of the drama and manipulation that others bring to it. And that's true not just in negotiations but also in relationships: in personal relationships, romantic relationships, business partnerships, the whole gamut. If you don't give energy to something, it must die out or shift. The only way something continues is if people continue to give it energy.

> **If you don't give energy to something, it must die out or shift. The only way something continues is if people continue to give it energy.**

Now, you may have noticed that, in the last paragraph, I said, "I really do practice what I preach . . . most of the time." No matter how much I negotiate and train people in this work, I am human, and occasionally I blow it as well. For example, about a year ago I received a call from someone representing a prior business partner from a business relationship I chose to end, for many reasons. From my point of view, that prior business partner had done a number of vindictive, unethical things triggered by my exit. I was still angry, upset, and frustrated. The person who called was hired after I had departed, didn't know me, didn't have full context as to all that happened, and had a view of me based upon the narrative he was told. In the beginning of the call, I got triggered, reactive, and angry and did not practice CDE at all. Despite catching myself in the middle of the call and readjusting, as you can imagine, it was not a good call. When I evaluated what went wrong after the fact, I observed the following:

1. I took the call on the fly. It was not scheduled so I did not prepare for it at all.

2. I had just come off another call with a client and didn't even have time to shift gears.

3. I hadn't worked through the lingering emotions I had built up inside and let them govern the interaction.

4. I certainly did not do a CPR or use any of the other tools I teach.

5. My state of being was not in the right place at all.

What should I have done? I should have refused the call when it came in and had my assistant schedule it for a later date. I then would have prepared for the call, worked through the anger I still felt, put a plan in place, done a CPR, and gotten myself into a state of CDE. I also would have stayed much more connected to the five steps to being a great negotiator.

So, with that admission and context, let's delve into the five steps.

1. CREATE AND STAY CONNECTED TO A POWERFUL CONTEXT.

Your context is the place you're coming from internally—your ground of being. You always have a context, whether it is created intentionally or is there by default and whether it is clearly distinguished or lurking in the murky subconscious. If you do not do the work to distinguish your existing context and, if necessary, to replace or reframe that context to something more empowering and useful, then you will not be successful in negotiating.

Let's imagine that you have been approached with a huge opportunity to sell your software to Google. This deal could be a game changer for you. You are excited and nervous going into the first negotiating session, which is natural. You do your external preparation in terms of deals Google has done in the past, who you're negotiating with, what distinguishes you, etc. But you still have this feeling of uneasiness. You have a choice: you can say, "Hey, it's natural to be nervous—this is Google! This is the biggest deal of my life!" or, you can choose to dig in and figure out deep down what context you're holding. Is it desperation for the deal? Are you feeling not good enough? Are you afraid of failure or of success? Do you think this opportunity came to you through sheer luck?

Once you determine the context you are holding, then you have an opportunity to change it to one that is true for you and more empowering. We will talk more about context later—how to create an empowering one and how to use that in preparing for negotiating when I discuss CPR.

For now, let me give some examples. Let's say you are going into a negotiation around a deal that it is unlikely that you are going to get. Maybe you're that start-up company negotiating with Google to buy your software. You've never done a deal with a large company before, and this is your first negotiating session with Google. If you hold the context of "I need to sell this software to them," then you can walk out of that if you don't get the sale and say, "I lost that negotiation. That session was a failure." Going into that negotiation session with the desperation or needy energy that this context brings will not only significantly decrease your chances of getting the deal but is also likely to reduce your ability to see other opportunities and gain other insights that might be available from the experience.

But if you go into that negotiation with a context of learning, for example, it is a whole different game: "It's an opportunity for me to learn because I know based upon a lot of people I've spoken to who have been successful in doing enterprise-level software deals, that sometimes it takes ten, twenty, or fifty meetings with various companies to get your first deal." If you treat this as a learning experience rather than as a life-or-death situation, then you're coming from a much calmer, more positive and empowering place: "I'm going to attempt to negotiate a deal in which Google buys my software. I am in a place of Detachment as to whether they do or don't. Whether I get the deal or not, one of the things I want to get out of this negotiation or the context I'm holding is to learn something that'll help me the next time."

Some people jump too quickly to try to close a deal. Sometimes at the first meeting around a potential deal or contract or whatever it is you're going to be negotiating, the context might be building a relationship. Certainly, when you're dealing with people from certain cultures you may find that they move more slowly, as compared to the American large city approach, which often is to jump right into business. There are many cultures in the world in which that's considered rude, and the first time or two you get together you shouldn't talk business at all. You just build a relationship. If you are holding a context of closing the deal, as opposed to building a relationship or having patience, then you will not be successful.

Another example: say you're an executive who's approached by a recruiter regarding a job that a potential employer wants to offer you. You know there will be a negotiation over salary and benefits and vacation, but you're probably not going to discuss those the first time around. You want to meet and build the relationship with the other side and make sure you're comfortable before you do that deal. So your context for that first meeting may be to build a relationship. Another context could be mutual respect and dignity. There are many different empowering contexts you can hold, but if your context is "I need this job" or "I am intimidated by this CEO," then you are not going to get the best results. The work involved is not to let the ego convince you that "you have this" without doing the internal work or to prevent you from admitting that the context you are really holding deep inside is one of the disempowering ones.

When I talk about context, many people ask about win–win. I agree with the idea of win–win; if you have any kind of negotiation with an ongoing relationship, you don't want to have one side win absolutely and the other side totally lose. The problem is that win–win itself has become a tactic. People say, "I really want this to be a win–win situation," and then proceed to beat their opponents up, manipulate them, try to crush them, and get the most they can. If it is a tactic to try to get what you want, to lure the other side into a false sense of security, it is not effective, and it comes across as disingenuous. Also, for some, the minute you introduce the concept of winning, their ego engages. So what I say is that win–win can be powerful as a context—meaning that if you relate to it on the level of being, it can be powerful, but only if it truly speaks to you and you can hold it as a true context.

2. BE WILLING TO DO WHAT IT TAKES TO GET TO YOUR TRUTH.

We all lie to ourselves sometimes, but if we do that going into a negotiation, then we're likely to find that we haven't done the necessary preparation to be successful. Often this happens because we didn't want to deal with whatever we needed to deal with to get to our truth. As we discussed, Clarity is the first key part of CDE; if you don't get Clarity in the beginning, then you'll waste a lot of time and design your negotiating strategy based on a false foundation. If you don't do adequate preparation, then you don't dig down deep enough to know what you really want. Then, when push comes to shove and you suddenly bring up a new point, the other side is liable to conclude that you're playing games with them, and you will lose credibility. That's why it's critical to do that internal work early on to get that level of clarity so that you don't end up in a compromised position.

So, how do you do what it takes to get to your truth? First, give yourself the gift of time and space to get clear. Many of us neglect to allow ourselves the kind of time required, because we're all so busy. You're running from meeting to meeting, you're handling your various obligations. Taking a day or even an

Give yourself the gift of time and space to get clear.

hour off to do a visioning session, or simply to take a step back and think, might seem like time you don't have—but if you want negotiating success, then you need to make that time.

In the past, when I've needed to make that time for myself to get clear, I would often go up to my place at the lake to be alone for a day or two. I'd shut off my devices and be 100 percent focused. But it doesn't always require that I spend a day or weekend away for me to get my clarity; depending on the level of negotiation, it could simply be an hour of quiet time. It could be going out for a run and thinking about it; it could be meditating or praying. It's different for different people; it could be just taking the time to bounce ideas off of somebody you trust. It's really whatever helps you get to your truth and to a place of clarity. But a lot of us aren't willing to take the time, and so we end up winging it and being unprepared or underprepared.

Don't let your ego or your fear stop you from digging deep. All of us have deep-rooted limiting beliefs and disempowering paradigms that can hold us back. I am committed to continuously working on myself, to always be growing personally and professionally. The more personal and professional growth you do, particularly the kind of inner work we're discussing here, the more prepared you will be to do what it takes to get to your truth in negotiating anything in your life. To me, Bob Proctor has been one of the most influential masters of teaching about paradigms and how to break through them. For more information about Proctor's work and other resources to help you get to your truth by identifying and transforming limiting beliefs, go to www.coreykupfer.com/resources.

3. IDENTIFY AND FULLY OWN YOUR OWN VALUE.

One of the biggest issues you may deal with is setting your prices and determining whether you're willing to negotiate those prices: What do I charge for what I do, whether it's a service or it's providing a product? That up-front pricing decision is the biggest factor in shaping how you will handle the inevitable negotiations later with customers, clients, distributors, and other stakeholders.

We've all run up against a situation in which somebody wants to negotiate to reduce our rates or our prices. The first piece is determining your prices up front. Do you charge $100 an hour or $500 an hour or $1,000 an hour? Do you charge $1,000, $2,500 or $5,000 for this project or product?

The next piece is what happens if somebody wants to renegotiate your rates or your terms, the amount of time you have to put in, the quality or quantity of goods, or any other aspect of your proposal. What it really takes to protect yourself from getting beaten up in those negotiations, or to strengthen your resolve not to cave in when you really shouldn't, is to first identify and fully own your value.

When you know you're going to deliver value at least equal to what you charge, then you're in a great place.

How do you decide what your work, product, or time is actually worth? What I would suggest to you is that you need to gather information. Look at what the market is, what your competitors are doing, and at the feedback you're getting from your customers. But then you need to look inside. Establish your own fair value, at a number you can stand for, not from a place of upset or ego if somebody tries to negotiate it, and not from a place of scarcity, but a place of 100 percent ownership of the value you bring. When you know you're going to deliver value at least equal to what you charge, then you're in a great place.

I don't negotiate my fees. When somebody says, "Can you discount?" I tell them, "No, I'm sorry. We don't do that. We very carefully consider how we price and what our rates are, and that's what we charge. We're confident we provide value at or beyond what we charge." We may change pricing if the client is willing to reduce the scope of services but not for the same scope. My view is that if I have to negotiate my rates or prices, I have not priced my services correctly in the first place. If your ego is too invested, then you can get angry or offended when someone asks about a discounted price, but if you're stating what you know your worth to be, then there's no reason to take offense; it's not as if I bang the table, with an "I'm not budging" kind of thing. Earlier in my career I didn't have the level of internal clarity and confidence and used to price lower and then negotiate down at times. Identifying and owning your value is a body of work that evolves over time.

When you're aware of your value and committed to getting what you're worth, that's a very calm, confident place in which to be. You have to trust your self-valuation because you need to be willing to let people who think you're too expensive walk away, and you have to have faith in the knowledge that there'll be other clients/customers coming your way down the line.

Nature abhors a vacuum; if you start cutting or negotiating your rates, taking less than you're worth, then you're going to fill your client ranks with lower-paying customers, and you won't have room left for those clients, customers, distributors, and business partners to come in at what you're really worth. You need to create that vacuum, and that's difficult because that vacuum may mean that you temporarily make less money. Maybe at the discounted price you're still making some profit, but you need to trust in your worth; create that vacuum and hold to it.

Again, this is not coming from a place of ego, because that won't attract what you need, but rather from a place of clarity that those clients, those customers, and those business partners will show up. You need to understand your USP—your unique selling proposition; what is it that makes you unique? What value-add are you providing? That allows you to first educate your prospective customer, then to negotiate.

I get calls from prospective new clients fairly frequently who say, "Corey, I want you to do x. What do you charge for that?" Mind you, this is before we build a relationship and before I've had any opportunity to explain our value proposition or how we work. It is before we've given the potential client or prospect any basis for evaluating us. If I answer that price question up front, all the client is doing is comparing me like a commodity against other people who have quoted her prices and rates. And yes, I might be able to tell her what my rate is, but as somebody who bills by the hour for certain work, the rate is only half the conversation. If I charge $800 an hour and somebody else charges $400, but it takes that person three times as long, then they're going to be more expensive. So you need to also know how long it's going to take to do the work contracted for, or, if it's a product or good, how quickly the client needs it. Do we have normal delivery time, or do we have to expedite the process? Do we have to put people on overtime to produce it? That may cost more.

That's why I never answer that question up front; it's not that I'm trying to avoid anything. I honestly and truthfully say to the person, "I'd be happy to discuss pricing with you, but I need more information first. Tell me more about what you are trying to accomplish. Tell me more about what you need me to do. Tell me more about what your objectives are." Then I ask more probing and specific questions related to their answers. I'm not trying to play games; I really can't give honest pricing unless I fully understand what they're trying to achieve and how I can help them do so. It also allows me to gather information from them about what's important to them, and it enables me to customize my proposal to their needs and then price it accordingly. That's something you want to do, not only to put yourself in a stronger negotiating position but also because it's part of having integrity and authenticity in business.

Very often in their eagerness to get the work, people will under-price themselves and then resent having done so later, and the person who winds up paying for that is almost always the customer. A common situation is one with which many of us are familiar—working with a building contractor. If you're contemplating a renovation, you might get three bids and pick the lowest bid. Too often, what happens then is that your contractor walks off the job when he's only halfway or three-quarters of the way through. He's run out of money because he underbid the job, and now he's not paying his subs. This happens for one of two reasons; the first might be that the person's a con artist and manipulator who figured that he or she would underbid it and then hit you with a bill for more later. There are some of those out there. But for a lot of them, it's just that they didn't ask the right questions and do enough due diligence. They honestly thought they could finish the job for the quoted price, and now they're slammed. They've gotten themselves into trouble and don't know how to dig out.

This is why getting clarity on what your value is, holding to it, and being able to educate the client or the customer on it is important. When they say, "So-and-so quoted me three-quarters of your price," then you're prepared to explain the reasons why to them: "Well, we do it this way that is different than the others. We're going to be available. Check our references. Did they ask you this question or that question? Did you detail these specs with them?" Differentiating yourself is a big part of identifying and fully owning your value. I'm

> **Differentiating yourself is a big part of identifying and fully owning your value.**

very comfortable that I'm charging what I'm worth, that I'm not ripping anybody off, that I'm going to give value that's at least equal to what I'm charging, because I have clarity. I can be calm and confident in that and not get thrown off if somebody tells me they won't work with me unless I cut my prices. I'm able to say, "I appreciate that. We're clearly not the right fit. You should use somebody else, and we wish you all the best," and I really mean it. I am able to say that because I have gotten to a place of Detachment. The other thing having Clarity allows you to do is to honor your moral compass and values every step of the way and to maintain your Equilibrium.

Take that contractor example, especially the one who just didn't do the work required up front in order to price the job correctly. There's this temptation when you get desperate to say, "All right, I've got to finish the job, but I really can't. So I'm going to save some costs here, save some costs there because I'm losing money on this job already." You avoid all of that temptation if you do things right up front and you simply stand and act in a moral way, not based upon external factors but based upon telling the truth. Yes, in setting your value, you're going to gather external information about what the competition's doing. But, ultimately, how and what you charge for your goods or services needs to come from a deep place internally, where you know inherently that the value you are providing matches or exceeds what you are charging somebody. It ultimately becomes somewhat irrelevant that the competition charges x or y. It is just a data point you're taking into account. If your competitor is charging a price you feel is higher than you're worth, then you can't raise your price to meet it, because you're not going to have the internal confidence in that number. If he's charging $500 an hour, and you don't feel comfortable with that, then you cannot look at somebody in the eye and confidently say, "I charge $500 an hour." You can only look confident when you say, "I charge $300 an hour." You're better off charging $300 an hour than $500 an hour because you're not going to be able to hold that and you're much less likely to get the customer. When somebody negotiates with you to reduce the higher rate, you're going to get thrown off or you're going to try to hold it from a place of upset and ego.

People respond positively when you are aligned, authentic, and comfortable with what you are proposing.

People respond positively when you are aligned, authentic, and comfortable with what you are proposing. That means that you will get a lot more business at $300 an hour if you can hold that in your being, than trying to get $500 an hour if you can't. Then the game plan becomes continuing to do the internal work so that you're ultimately able to hold $500 an hour.

There's a great story that I have heard Jack Canfield, the *Chicken Soup for the Soul* author, tell. As I remember it, Jack says that before he'd started writing books and making all kinds of money doing it, he was making four figures a year as a teacher. He started doing little talks for educators and at conferences, charging $400 per talk. He got into a conversation with a colleague and discovered that he was doing the same kinds of speaking engagements as Jack but charging

$1,200 for them. Jack's first reaction was, *How is this guy getting paid three times what I am when I'm better than he is?* Naturally, that made him reexamine his pricing and question his own value and worth. Could he charge that much? Was he worth it? So the next time he got on the phone and somebody said, "We want to hire you for a speaking engagement. What's your rate?" Jack said he was thinking of answering $1,200, but he couldn't really get himself to say it, so instead he quoted him $800.

The man said, "No problem."

Jack said, "Just out of curiosity what would have been a problem?"

The man told him, "We had $1,500 in the budget for the speaker." Jack honored the $800 price he'd quoted, but he had learned his lesson. The next phone call he got where somebody asked him to speak and asked him what his fee was, Jack said, "$1,500."

They said, "We only have $1,200 in the budget."

He said, "I'll take it."

As you can see, getting to the point at which he could hold to higher numbers was a process that he went through, as it is with most of us. As he got more and more comfortable, he got paid more and more money. Jack Canfield's teachings around how you manifest what you can envision are some of the best. I am also a fan of Wayne Dyer's work in this area. For more information and links to their work, go to www.coreykupfer.com/resources. This work of owning your value puts you in a much stronger position to negotiate all terms of the deal—not just money—delivery time, volume minimums, exclusivity, you name it.

4. ALWAYS BE IN INTEGRITY.

It's simple—always be in integrity. This one is nonnegotiable. (And, yes, I am banging the table—well not really because I advise against it, but this is important!) It's only necessary if you want to be successful, build strong relationships, and be happy (so, no pressure). Not only is the "honesty" part of integrity table-stakes (meaning, it should be a given) because, without trust, it's over; but the "being true to yourself" part of integrity—which is what I'm more concerned with here—is crucial to everything else. If you are not true to who you are, honoring your moral compass and acting from your internal truth, then how can you apply any of the other things you have learned from this book? How do you have Clarity if you are not connected to your inner truth? How can you attain a state of Detachment when your ego is engaged or you are afraid, which are two of the main reasons you get disconnected from your integrity? How can you stay in Equilibrium when the lack of alignment with your integrity will foster doubt, discomfort, and unease?

There are often temptations that call to us and might even provide us with short-term benefits, but succumbing to those temptations is never worth it. More often, though, good people end up out of integrity not because they make conscious choices to act out of alignment but rather because they have not been willing to do the hard work to get clear on, own, and trust what is in integrity for them. Their lack of clarity and connection leaves them with no compass, and only after they go down the wrong road for a while do they realize that something doesn't feel right. Then they have a thorny decision to make: do they turn back or—because they have so much invested and others have certain expectations—do they continue and compromise their values?

If you do the body of work to attain Clarity, Detachment, and Equilibrium fully, deeply, and completely, you will by definition be in alignment with your own integrity. You will be clear on where you stand, and you won't be swayed or turned from that place by societal paradigms, people's expectations, or other external forces. If you are in a negotiation and something feels out of integrity for you—even if you can't put it into words or identify the issue fully—take a step back, call a time-out, reconnect, and don't move forward with the negotiation (and, certainly, don't complete the negotiation) before you are sure that you are back in alignment with your integrity.

5. HAVE HIGH EXPECTATIONS.

It's crucial that you go into a negotiation with high expectations. In fact, that's true for anything in life, whether it's going into a meeting with your boss or meeting with a new client.

Top negotiators have high expectations. I'm not talking about pipe dreams or unreasonable outcomes: it's not, "I'm going to sell my company. It's really worth $1 million but I'm going to get $5 million." It's not about expecting something that is totally unrealistic. It is about having levelheaded expectations but also holding a high expectation that you will achieve what you want to get out of the negotiation.

Why is this important? When you have high expectations, you go in with a certain energy, with a confidence in how you relate to other people that makes your chances of being successful a lot higher. It's the opposite of being in that place of scarcity and fear. The majority of the way we communicate is not via our words—it is through our body language, tonality, and micro-facial expressions (of which there are many, and they are nearly impossible to control) that betray your underlying feelings to others. Go in with set expectations, not from an ego place but from an internally centered space, expecting a good result, and you will be in a much better place to get it done. There's a lot of talk about the law of attraction out there, thanks to the popularity of the book and movie *The Secret*. There's some controversy around whether this "law" is genuine; some people really believe it. Some people think it is a lot of bunk. I believe it in the way that Bob Proctor explains it, which is not what most people think it is—that what you think about, you attract.

What Proctor says is that the law of attraction is based on the law of vibration, so actually you get what you truly expect and believe in, not what you say.

What Proctor says is that the law of attraction is based on the law of vibration, so actually you get what you truly expect and believe in, not what you say. In other words, you could be thinking, *I'm going to attract a job to myself that pays $250,000*, or, *I'm going to attract a buyer for my company that's going to pay me $10 million.* Well, no. That's not enough. The thing is, if you're in a negative or doubtful vibration, if you truly don't believe that that's going to occur, but you're saying it to yourself, then you're not going to manifest it. It may be a good technique. Like a lot of people, I believe in affirmations because if you do affirmations, then eventually you actually start to believe what you're saying, even if you didn't believe it in the beginning. But if you're in a place where you're going into a negotiation saying, "I have high expectations. I'm going to close the deal at $10 million for my company," but what's really in your gut or in your heart is, "I'm never going to get $10 million for my business. I'm going to get $8 million at best," then that's ultimately what's going to play a big role in your outcome.

There are many studies of the positive impact of high expectations on results or what is often called the Pygmalion or Rosenthal effect, named after a Greek myth and the lead researcher in this area, respectively. For more information on these studies, go to www.coreykupfer.com/resources.

So when you do the work to get clarity, get that clarity while holding high expectations and then continue to hold those high expectations throughout the negotiation process.

The thing is to do the work; again, it could be through prayer or maybe through meditation. It could be getting your head clear through exercising. It could be through speaking to people whom you trust. Some people are much more analytical, and if this is you, you can run spreadsheets and analyze what other companies sold for, so you can get comfortable with the idea that it's fair and reasonable to expect your price. This process looks different for everybody. But if you do the work to get to the point where your vibration or your confidence—your inner energy—aligns with the understanding that your position is fair and reasonable rather than something you're just saying to yourself, then that's when you're able hold high expectations and have more success.

A lot of people can go into negotiations with high expectations, but then in the battle or the back-and-forth of the negotiation, they get thrown off. They start losing confidence, and they don't hold those high expectations anymore. They don't maintain their equilibrium. That gives off messages to the other side that can be very detrimental to a successful negotiation.

When you create and stay connected to a powerful context, do what it takes to get to your truth, identify and fully own your value, and are in integrity—that's what makes it possible for you to have and hold high expectations. Do these five things—achieve and maintain Clarity, Detachment, and Equilibrium and use the CPR framework—and your negotiating success will increase significantly.

> **Do these five things— achieve and maintain Clarity, Detachment, and Equilibrium and use the CPR framework—and your negotiating success will increase significantly.**

In the final two chapters, I will discuss CPR in a lot more detail. It is a great framework for preparing yourself to be at your most centered, powerful, and effective when you sit down at that table across from your opponents. But first, let's look at some inauthentic negotiation tactics and techniques and how to handle them from a CDE approach.

CHAPTER FIVE

INAUTHENTIC NEGOTIATING TECHNIQUES AND HOW TO HANDLE THEM

As you see by now, there is a huge difference between the way many of us have been taught to deploy tactics and techniques to disarm, mislead, get leverage over or scare our opponents, and authentic negotiating. Since many others still try to use these tactics and techniques, we must know what they are and how to deal with them.

So what are the classic inauthentic techniques? You can find a list of tactics and techniques pulled from websites, books, training programs, and other sources and suggestions and videos on how to deal with them at www.coreykupfer.com/resources. For now, let's run through just a few of these techniques in more detail, talk a little about what they are, how and when they work, and what the authentic negotiating approach is to them.

The Empty Promise: An agreement has been made, and a promise given; for instance, "We will pay you x dollars, if you agree to this." It's not uncommon that people will just throw out a number that's higher than other bidders for the company, the deal, or the product or lower for the project or service, just to be the ones who win the bid, even though when they're offering that amount they know it's an empty promise. They know they're going to find a reason some time later on to reduce the price or increase the fee, and they're going to blame it on something they found in, for example, due diligence or some alleged change in circumstances.

Now, there are cases in which someone does due diligence and might uncover some previously unknown information that makes it appropriate, for example, to adjust a purchase price. But in using the tactic I'm talking about here, whatever they found or whatever they claim or whatever the change in circumstances they say exists, it isn't really the case. They knew all along that they would never be willing to pay what they offered up front. So, what do you do in that circumstance? The first thing you don't do is get upset, make accusations, or let this tactic throw you off. You reconnect to CDE and especially focus on staying Detached. If you calmly say that the change doesn't work for you and ask them to reconsider the change, you will be surprised how many times they will back down. They may test you and try to trigger you first by insisting the circumstances have changed but, if you don't take the bait, it will be on them to either cave or lose the deal.

The Big Fish: This tactic is used when one company is much larger and more powerful than the other in a negotiation, and the larger company presumes it can intimidate the smaller one. Let's say an innovative entrepreneurial company comes up with a new product, a disruptive product that has potential to change a marketplace. That makes them an attractive acquisition target for the bigger companies who don't innovate as quickly. The big company will often make an offer; if the smaller company is not receptive, what's lingering in the background and sometimes comes to the forefront is, "Hey listen, either you do the deal with us or we'll put you out of business. You should be happy that we're willing to buy you because we're a multibillion-dollar company and you're not." This can play out on a smaller scale too, as long as there is a large relative size difference. The gist of the message is always the same, however: "If you don't sell to us, we'll develop this on our own or we'll buy someone else, and we'll make it our business to crush you."

This can, of course, backfire; founders can get their backs up when the would-be buyer tries the Goliath act. There are many situations in which founders have turned down these buyers and later done a lot better. That's not always the way it shakes out, of course, but it very easily can put off the people who you ought to be wooing, not bullying.

Remember, even if you are the small fish, you always have leverage (nobody has no leverage) in that you can walk away from the deal if it doesn't meet your criteria. Also, if you keep your equilibrium, this bullying should not affect you emotionally, and you can calmly explain your value proposition and why the big fish is better off buying you or doing a deal with you than with someone else or doing it themselves. This is a much more effective approach than getting triggered or afraid. Remember to trust and that the only thing worse than no deal is a bad deal.

> **Remember to trust and that the only thing worse than no deal is a bad deal.**

Nibbling: It's appropriate in negotiations to put the areas or categories of what will be discussed in the negotiation on the table up front (although not necessarily your position on every issue) because no one term can be negotiated in a vacuum. You've perhaps heard the saying, "Name a price, and I'll give you a structure. Name a structure, and I'll give you a price." That's a great example: whether you want to pay me $1.0 million or $1.2 million, it makes a big difference as to whether I'm getting it up front or I'm getting it over ten years, for example. All of the major terms should be on the table, even if there's room to negotiate in each of them.

Nibbling is when people give you their comments, you go through a negotiation and you think you're getting close to figuring out the issues and then they say, "You know what, I have these three other concerns I haven't mentioned before." The next time you get on the phone with them or you sit down with them, they bring up another two points that they hadn't previously put on the table. You've already negotiated your position in the first round or two based on what you thought was the whole list of issues, so you gave in on this in exchange for that, etc., and now all of the sudden you must factor in all of these new issues. Had you known about those previously undisclosed issues up front—that they were going to ask you for these additional three or four things—then you wouldn't have agreed to make certain concessions in the first couple of rounds.

So how do you handle people who are nibbling? My recommendations are the first time they come back and add additional requests, from a place of Detachment and Equilibrium, you point out that these are new terms and that your prior agreements will need to be reevaluated in light of them. Then ask whether these are the final additional items. Make it clear that if there are any others, they should let you know now, as you are not willing to negotiate piecemeal, because you need to consider the deal as a whole to be able to evaluate it properly. Confirm to them that you have set forth all of your requests so that you model the behavior and are in integrity in requiring the same from them. Then objectively analyze the additional requests, and determine whether they are acceptable or not from a place of CDE and what, if anything, you agreed to previously might need to be reevaluated in light of their new demands.

The Quivering Quill: The "quill" in this phrase refers to an old-fashioned pen. Here's how it works: You have gone through the negotiation process, you think everything has been covered and agreed on, and it is time to sign off on the deal. You're in the closing room together, and you may literally have the pen in your hand ready to sign the agreement, when suddenly the other side says, "Hey, before we close this deal, there's one other thing we need." I've seen this tactic play out many times, in many situations; at the last minute, there's a request for a concession, and someone saying, "We will not sign unless . . ."

Admittedly, this can be an "effective" ploy: if you're the one using it, you're counting on the momentum that the other party has toward getting the deal done to push him past his resistance to this last-ditch demand. Very often, it puts the other party in a tight spot because he has a lot invested and is coming into the closing with the assumption that this deal is, for all intents and purposes, already done. He might be badly embarrassed or worse should it all suddenly go south. It will likely be seen as being terribly manipulative, though, and if you have overestimated the importance to the other party of closing the deal, it will backfire.

When someone tries to run the Quivering Quill on you, it's easy for this tactic to trigger your ego and anger, hurt, or frustration. Instead of getting thrown off by this ploy, go back to your preparation, practice CDE, and refer back to your CPR. Calmly evaluate whether this last-minute concession would have been acceptable if it had been asked for earlier, based on your CPR and connecting to your clarity. If the answer is no, then check to make sure you're still Detached from the outcome and that you're maintaining your Equilibrium, and then decline to agree to the new term. Calmly let the other party know that if they want to close the deal, then they need to withdraw their last-minute request. Alternately, if after that evaluation you determine that the new point is one to which you would have agreed had it been presented to you earlier, then you know you can agree to it now. That does not mean that you will, but you know you have options. You can agree so you get the deal done; you can ask for a concession in exchange; you can decide not to agree because the request came so late or because you don't want to establish a pattern of agreeing to last-minute concessions, especially in an ongoing relationship. But the key thing is that you are making that decision from a place of Clarity, Detachment, and Equilibrium.

If this is the type of deal that involves what will be an ongoing business partnership or other close relationship, you may want to consider whether their use of this tactic, or any of the other manipulative tactics, means you need to reevaluate whether you really want to be in business with this person. Is it a breach of trust? It may warrant an open conversation about that. Before you jump to a lot of negative conclusions, however, keep in mind that just because people are badly trained as negotiators doesn't necessarily mean they are bad people or business partners. Also, be aware that this is much more commonplace and acceptable in some cultures than it is in others. If asking for a last-minute concession is just part of your counterpart's cultural style, then it may not be an indicator of bad character. To repeat an earlier point, if you're dealing with someone whose national or cultural background is different from yours, it will serve you well to do the necessary research ahead of your negotiation so that you'll be prepared for the differences in negotiating style that you may encounter or need to employ.

> If asking for a last-minute concession is just part of your counterpart's cultural style, then it may not be an indicator of bad character.

Limited Authority: Have you ever been in a negotiation where the person you're talking to stops the conversation because they claim that they have to check with someone above them, in order to get authority to make the concession you've requested? This does a number of things: it can shake your certainty that the request you've made is a legitimate one; it delays the agreement, putting pressure on you to speed things up, possibly by waiving your request; and it brings in the specter of greater powers outside of the room who are actually running the negotiation—powers you can't see or know. Even worse, in some cases, it is not true— it is just being used as a false tactic.

So what are some of the things you can do to deal with the limited authority ploy? There are some who recommend asking up front whether the person has authority to do the deal. Although this may be appropriate in certain circumstances, this is often not the best way to go, because even if the person you are talking to does not have ultimate authority, they are likely to have some influence and may serve as a gatekeeper. If you insult them or make them feel unimportant, you may never get to the person with the authority. This is especially true if you approach the conversation from a place of ego, upset, or superiority. There is a big difference between challenging someone on their authority and, for example, having someone on your team inquire who will be at the table on the other side so that he or she knows who to bring from their team. Is this a preliminary meeting, or are we bringing the decision-makers to try to get this locked up? The mutuality of the conversation changes it from a challenge or potential insult to an approach of working together and coordinating for best results.

Doing your preparation work will help you understand who has authority. Know in advance what the organizational structure of the company across the table is, try to determine who have been the key players in prior similar business deals, and ask up front who will be in the room with you, working out the deal.

Know in advance what the organizational structure of the company across the table is, try to determine who have been the key players in prior similar business deals, and ask up front who will be in the room with you, working out the deal.

THE PROBLEM WITH THE TACTIC/COUNTERTACTIC GAME

One problem with all of these tactics is that you have to assume that the other party is as familiar with them as you are—and that they're also aware of how to counter these manipulative gambits. The negotiation can easily degenerate into a back-and-forth game of tactics, countertactics, countertactics to the countertactics, *ad nauseum*. If someone's trying the Big Fish routine, for instance, a negotiator might use the "I Have Other Suitors" countertactic. If you're a software start-up and you are negotiating with Google or Microsoft, who tell you, "Hey, sell to me or I'm going to crush you," a tactic would be to tell them, "You should know that I'm negotiating with your competitor as well. You won't crush us. We'll go to one of the other big boys. They're interested." They can come back and try to call your bluff. You then can lie about the status of negotiations with the competitor. You can see how this exchange can deteriorate into a disingenuous, manipulative game with no winners, or, even if a deal gets done, create a business relationship built on an inauthentic base.

Empty promises can be countered in a number of ways. You can bang the table and demand that they stick to the original terms. Another response I've seen is to get angry and call them out on their lack of integrity, to bluster and counterattack. Some people simply get up and walk out. But again, this is just a cycle of games and inauthenticity.

One sometimes-effective way to counter the nibbling technique is the "Nibble Back" tactic. If they ask you for three concessions, ask them for three concessions. Some people simply counter this with anger or bluster, as well. Depending on the circumstances, another approach would be the "Appeal to a Higher Authority" tactic—it depends on who's asking for the concession—but if it's somebody who works for a firm, you can say, "I want to speak to your boss because this is unethical; I'm going to go above your head."

I could go on and on with examples of countertactics to tactics and counter-countertactics to countertactics but, of course, that is not the way to go. So, in addition to the specific ways I have already discussed, how do you counter-tactics like this without resulting to equally disingenuous or inauthentic ploys? One of my favorite ways is to just name the tactic. It takes the power right out of it. If you're in a room with two people, and one is being supportive and the other is being combative, you can ask, "Are you guys doing Good Cop, Bad Cop on me?" Ask it with a smile. You get a very different result when you ask that question from a calm, almost-amused place as though you're merely curious, rather than reacting with anger, which would reveal that you'd allowed their tactic to fluster or goad you.

For additional videos and tips on how to deal with other inauthentic tactics and techniques, visit www.coreykupfer.com/resources.

TELLS

There is another area of negotiating training and practice I have issues with, as well. This derives from training that can be useful in terms of how to read other people in a negotiation—how to interpret their "tells," as they call them at the poker table.

I talked a little earlier on in this book about how much we reveal about our inner feelings without being aware of it, especially when we're under stress. Whether it's through our body language, the tone of our voice, or our micro-facial expressions, really good negotiators will read those, accurately assess our emotional state, and potentially exploit that to manipulate us. Many negotiators are confident in their ability to mask their underlying feelings in a negotiation, relying on putting on a "poker face" they're sure their opposition will find impossible to read. But no experienced negotiator can be fooled that easily.

Additionally, there are other kinds of tells that we pick up on subliminally. You have probably experienced this: someone is saying something, but while what they're saying sounds good, somehow it doesn't *feel* right, and for reasons you might find hard to explain, you don't trust them. Eighty to 85 percent of the way we communicate is not in the words we say but rather in the signals we give off. A good negotiator will read these accurately and act accordingly. Someone who isn't so skilled will also get those signals because the ability to receive them is hardwired into us—but they won't respond to them properly. Maybe they're afraid of losing the deal, and they're coming from a place of scarcity; perhaps they're afraid of losing their job if they don't do the deal, so they'll start ignoring or rationalizing those uneasy feelings. This is a dangerous error; those feelings are powerful messages coming to you via instinct, and you can't afford to ignore them.

Whether it's through our body language, the tone of our voice, or our micro-facial expressions, really good negotiators will read those, accurately assess our emotional state, and potentially exploit that to manipulate us.

It's perilously easy to ignore signals, however—especially if you have a lot going on in the moment: the stress of the negotiation, your own concerns that you've brought into the room with you, or the sense that a great deal hinges on what happens. Alternately, if you're in a calm place, and your head is not all over the place, then you're going to get that sense of whether or not the person speaking is telling you the truth or trying to snow you, and you can use that information accordingly. Teaching this is not my area of expertise (so I will not be covering it further in this book).

There is some useful work in this area, and it would be worth checking out. There are those who can teach you how to read people and recognize tells, and that is useful. My issue is when trainers turn this around to train people on tactics and techniques around masking or hiding these tells. In my view, this is like prescribing medicine that tries to hide the symptoms of a disease but doesn't cure the underlying cause. Instead of asking how we mask or hide these tells, wouldn't it be more productive to determine why you are giving off the counterproductive signals in the first place?

The reason always comes down to the issues I've explored earlier in this book: factors such as fear, scarcity, and ego. If you are nervous, then your behavior will expose that. If you are afraid of losing the deal, your body language will reveal that fear. I would argue that if in fact those feelings are present, no matter what you do to try to hide or mask them, you'll never be able to fully conceal them. So how do we deal with these feelings that threaten to undermine us despite our best efforts to hide them?

What you don't feel, you don't reveal, and your body language, tone, and facial expressions will project that calm and certainty.

The knack, as exemplified by Mike in chapter 1, is being able to distance yourself from those complicating and ultimately useless emotions and thoughts and put yourself wholly in the moment. For an example of what that looks like, watch the movie *The Legend of Bagger Vance*. When the great golfer is in the zone, he sees nothing of what's going on around him. He is not conscious of the tension that others are feeling; he just sees the fairway, the green, and the hole. He tunes out the crowd, and he tunes out the chatter in his head. He tunes out any negative thoughts, and he is simply fully present in the moment. What you don't feel, you don't reveal, and your body language, tone, and facial expressions will project that calm and certainty.

MIRRORING

People have been trying to "game" the whole body language piece for a long time, and a technique that is talked about a lot is what's called "mirroring," which is pitched as a way to make the person with whom you're interacting feel more comfortable. How it works is that basically you imitate, or mirror, whatever the other person's doing. If the other person leans back, then you lean back. If the other person crosses her legs, then you cross the leg on the same side. If you're with a person who leans toward you, then you lean toward them. This is intended to create some sort of synergy and a sense of connection. While it can in fact accomplish that, the mirroring technique also often has the opposite effect, especially if it is used on somebody with any sophistication.

Here's the thing. If you are really listening to somebody, genuinely connecting with them, and actually do care about what they have to say, then you will mirror them. Mirroring is a human trait that we all do naturally; you're not consciously thinking about it, you're just doing it. The problem is that it's taught as a technique, which immediately renders it inauthentic. Once it is consciously applied, it no longer comes from a place of just being present, being clear, listening, or being connected. It comes from a place of tactics. You can get trained in this, and some people get pretty good, good enough perhaps to fool an unsophisticated person who may not catch on that it's being done purposefully. There are a lot of people who are really bad at it, though—embarrassingly so. And even those people who are good at it can be spotted as fakes by an experienced negotiator. The fact is, the minute you have to think about it, you change the dynamic. Somebody leans in, you think, *Oh, I should lean in,* and you lean in; it's very different than the actual way in which you would lean in if you were truly connected to them.

The work I do with negotiators is all about avoiding these kinds of awkward and inauthentic moments. Instead of working to master mirroring or controlling your body language, modulating your tone, or controlling your facial expressions, take all of that energy and put it into CDE. If you attain and maintain Clarity, Detachment, and Equilibrium, then you will never have to worry about your body language, your voice, or your facial expressions, because the place you will be in—your state of being—will give off all of the right signals. You will project clarity, confidence, calmness, lack of attachment, and centeredness, and your voice, body, and face will, too.

Having said that, tactics can work, and some people train so extensively in them that they become masters. Let's say that you are one of them; you know every single tactic and countertactic to each tactic. These can give you an advantage, even if you are deficient in the real underlying strengths: clarity, fearlessness, freedom from ego, etc., and you don't practice CDE when you're up against someone who is less skilled but similarly deficient. But it won't matter how masterful you are at the tactics; you're not going to be as successful against somebody who has done the external and the internal work to fully be in the state that Clarity, Detachment, and Equilibrium provides.

If, however, you've done that preparation and you work to master CDE, then you can take some of the non-manipulative techniques and tactics and have those in your arsenal. I'm not talking about Quivering Quill or anything as inauthentic as that, but there are some techniques and frameworks (such as being able to read other people's tells or being willing to sit comfortably in the silence) that may be appropriate and with which you may feel comfortable—ones that have integrity to you. But they have to be an addition to, not a substitute for, the tougher and far more important work of practicing CDE and negotiating authentically.

CHAPTER SIX

CPR—A NEGOTIATION-SAVING FRAMEWORK

've talked about the importance of entering a negotiation from a place of CDE: Clarity, Detachment, and Equilibrium. Now, let's talk about the most powerful methodological framework of which I am aware to help achieve and maintain that state: the internal preparation process of CPR—Context, Purpose, and Results. Probably the best way to introduce it is to show how it works in action in a specific case in which I helped clients to apply it to their own situation.

In this negotiation, I was representing a very significant team of multibillion-dollar clients in a service industry. They had entered into a deal with a firm that they had become affiliated with some years earlier. I had not represented them in that deal. Now, the relationship was not working out. They wanted to be able take their clients and go elsewhere.

When we looked at their legal agreements, it was clear that their legal position was weak. Basically, according to the terms of the agreement, they had given up rights to ownership of their client base; the company they had gone to effectively owned their clients. There were numerous restrictive covenants—meaning noncompetition and nonsolicit provisions. In other words, if they left, they couldn't solicit their client base to come with them. Mind you, they had gotten paid millions of dollars in this deal, so it's not as if they had received nothing for it, but now they wanted out and wanted to take their clients with them; the question was how would we get them there?

In some ways, we were negotiating without much leverage. In other ways, practically speaking, we had some leverage because in that kind of business, people most often have relationships with the individuals they work with, as opposed to the institution. Practically, if the clients left, even if they weren't allowed to take their clients with them, those clients might still go elsewhere, so the firm might lose them anyway. Plus, there was reputational risk on both sides if this went public, and we did have some legal arguments we could make on the client's behalf in terms of the employer's misrepresentations and breaches of contract. There were numerous factors at play.

Most importantly, though, my clients, who were very smart people and very capable people, had never been in this situation before. There was a lot of emotion involved. They felt that they had been duped into making the move to that company. They felt that their business had suffered because of promises that hadn't been kept and the lack of capabilities that were supposed to have been there but were not, along with a list of other factors that adversely affected them in providing an acceptable level of service to their clients. They were upset about this. There were also significant personality conflicts between my clients and the executives at the firm with which they were affiliated; they just didn't get along, and they didn't like each other.

Clearly, there was a lot in the mix that could make this into a volatile situation. Out of the two lead people (Lenny and Gina) in my client group, although they were both upset, Lenny was especially triggered and angry. I could see that anger could present a problem if we couldn't find a way to help him to keep his primary objectives in mind and hold his temper.

We had a whole legal strategy that we designed separately; in fact, we even had a significant legal complaint drafted and ready to be filed in court as a plan B if these negotiations should fail. You may be familiar with a negotiation theory with the acronym BATNA, which was developed at Harvard Program on Negotiation (PON) by researchers Roger Fisher and William Ury, who wrote a series of books on what they called "principled negotiation." The acronym BATNA refers to Best Alternative to a Negotiated Agreement, which is basically your plan B, the course of action you'll take if you fail to resolve your legal differences in negotiation.

In this case, our best alternative to the negotiated agreement was to commence a lawsuit. It wasn't a great alternative, but it was our strongest alternative, especially as opposed to the company filing one against my clients first. We had the legal complaint ready to go and had somebody sitting at the courthouse ready to file it if things went bad in the negotiating session that was scheduled to happen in Dallas on a particular day, despite the fact that none of us wanted it to happen. It was crucial to my clients that they come out of this with a negotiated deal, but they weren't willing to get out at any cost either. They would have litigated if they couldn't get an acceptable deal, but although we had some legitimate claims, we didn't love the odds of winning. So having a successful negotiation was crucial.

The question was, how could I best prepare Lenny and Gina to have a successful negotiation? While it would have been easy to jump into, "What do we want? What do they want? What's nonnegotiable? What are our strategies and tactics to get there?" Instead I applied the CDE methodology and CPR framework I teach and use myself in negotiations. This was especially important to this case because I knew that if we didn't do the underlying work, the stakes were so high, and there was so much emotion and tension involved and so much negative history with these parties, that it could all blow up. If I couldn't get them to a place of Clarity, Detachment, and Equilibrium, the negotiation never could be successful.

After creating the context of CDE for them, the first thing I taught Lenny and Gina to do was the CPR process. This is a powerful framework based on a similar approach I first learned about as a volunteer with the Hunger Project many years ago and was then again exposed to in some men's work I participated in for many years. I've adapted and redesigned it based on my own experience and applied it to negotiating amongst other things.

I explained, "We need to get clear not only on what we want, meaning the outcomes—the intended results. But even more importantly, we have to get clear on our purpose—what our 'why' is in this negotiation, and on the Context, meaning the state of being you need to be in to achieve that Purpose." Without that, I told them, I thought their chances of having a successful negotiation and not ending up in litigation were small. Fortunately, Lenny and Gina bought into it and were willing to trust and listen to me. So I worked with them to create their CPR.

A key piece of the CPR process is that it must be expressed in meaningful words, words that are crafted and "owned" by the individuals involved. These words matter because they have to speak to the people creating them; thus, while I could help them come up with that text and make suggestions for what they might want it to include, they ultimately couldn't be my words. They had to be *their* words— words that Lenny and Gina could reconnect to and get regrounded in, to bring themselves back to a place of calm and clarity—a place of CDE.

> A key piece of the CPR process is that it must be expressed in meaningful words, words that are crafted and "owned" by the individuals involved.

What we talked about initially was, what was the Context they're holding at that moment? Up until then, I had heard a lot of negativity—how it was a terrible place, how it was a bad partnership, how horrible the people/executives at the company were, how their clients didn't trust the company based upon a list of "evidence" that Lenny, Gina, and their other partners had, and about why their view of these people and their lack of trustworthiness was what it was.

I said to them, "If we had to describe the context you're holding right now, it's probably something around anger and lack of trust. It is reactionary. It is pessimistic." They agreed. I then said, "If you really are holding that context, what are the odds of having a successful negotiation sitting across the table from them, given your assumption that these guys are not trustworthy? You're going in with the mind-set that they're bad people, you don't like them, and you're pessimistic about being able to get a deal done with them. Given that mind-set, what are the odds you're going to get a deal that works for you?"

"Not very good," Gina said, and although he quickly agreed, Lenny went on to say, "But listen, it's true, these guys are not trustworthy. They lied to us." He then began to repeat all of the reasons they had for their view and starting getting into their evidence again.

"Wait, stop!" I said. "Lenny, you have a choice—do you want to be right, or do you want to be effective? If you want to be right, okay, but you won't be successful in this negotiation. If you want to be successful, then you need to give up being right. That doesn't mean that there isn't truth in what you are saying, it just means that holding that energy and focus will not be productive."

"Okay, I get it," he said. "I'm listening."

I continued, "Now that we know what won't work for you, what would be a more productive Context to hold to make this negotiation work; to achieve your Purpose and get the Results you want?" Dawn broke; Lenny's energy shifted, and smiles came to both of their faces—they now understood how they needed to shift their Context to have any chance at success. Before we dug in to determine exactly what their Context should be, I suggested, "Let's figure out what your Purpose is first."

With this CPR framework, the order in which you create it doesn't matter, whether it's Context first, Purpose, Results, the reverse, or whatever. It's simply a question of personal preference; when people apply it, they can do whatever way works best for them. Personally, I generally prefer to determine the Purpose first because the Purpose is the "why," and that "why," for me, influences everything else. Why are we entering into this negotiation? Next, I determine what the Context is that I need to hold to achieve that Purpose. Who do I need to be to achieve that Purpose?

Lastly, I figure out what the specific intended Results are, and that's usually the easiest part, especially after getting clear on the Context and Purpose: I want *x* dollars, and/or *x* time for delivery—

that's the nuts and bolts. It's important to get 100 percent clear on what your desired Results are, but that's usually the only place people go when thinking about an anticipated negotiation. The real work is in the Context and the Purpose.

I worked with Gina and Lenny to determine and clarify their Purpose. When you're starting this process, it may seem unclear, but, in fact, subconsciously there's always a Context there and there's always a Purpose. It may not be identified, it may not be clear in your mind, but it is present nonetheless. Had they gone into this negotiation without preparation, then their Purpose might have been to just beat the other side at all costs, to get revenge, or to show that they were right. None of those things were going to make them successful.

In working with them and determining what they wanted in their case, the first point was that they had received millions of dollars when they came in. They knew they were going to have to write a large check in order to leave. Gina and Lenny were okay with that because they knew they were going to take a lot of business with them, but the fact remained that they would have to pay a significant amount of money in order to be free of this relationship. So that's where we began: Was their Purpose to pay as little as possible? Was their Purpose around timing?

As it turned out, when we discussed it in depth, the money was less important to them than they'd initially thought. What they finally determined was that they just wanted out. Their Purpose was to exit the company and to take their clients with them.

Now, phrased that way, that's very reactionary; "I just want out." That led us to the question of what an empowering expression of that Purpose would be—something that they could go back to which would ground them when things got tough. The Purpose that they came to with my help and a lot of deep thinking, internal honesty, and work to gain Clarity was to "Get our freedom back." Simple? Yes. Empowering, certainly. For Lenny and Gina, it was inspiring. Getting our freedom back; that's a meaningful goal to work toward. In fact, when they hit on the word "freedom," that clinched it; that really resonated with them. I remember Gina practically yelling, "Yes, freedom, that's it!" Think about it; when you are in a tough negotiation, you must weigh your potential outcomes; is your goal to get out with as much of your money intact as possible, or is it, in fact, to be free of your toxic partners?

> "Will my reaction, will the next thing I say or do, move me closer to or further away from getting our freedom back?' That's the only test. Is it going to move you closer to getting our freedom back? If so, that's good. Go ahead. If it's not, don't do it, don't say it."

Ultimately, their larger Purpose was to get their freedom back, which for them included getting out with their client base intact. Freedom needed to include the freedom to take their clients, along with the freedom to move on.

I said to them, "You need to be prepared to react to what they're going to throw at you. When somebody on the other side who you really don't like says something and you get triggered and you're about to react—whether it's out of anger, whether it's out of frustration, or whether it's because you know you're right—then you're going to ask yourselves this question: 'Will my reaction, will the next thing I say or do, move me closer to or further away from getting our freedom back?' That's the only test. Is it going to move you closer to getting our freedom back? If so, that's good. Go ahead. If it's not, don't do it, don't say it."

You can imagine being in that kind of highly charged emotional situation, where somebody says something and you want to react because you feel you're right. Maybe you *are* right. But if you think about it, if your Purpose is clear, then what you'll say to yourself is, "Wait a second; yes, I'm right, but will my being right only trigger them to get more defensive? If so, it won't move me closer to getting my freedom back. Do I really need to be right in this moment? Is there a different direction I can take? Is there a different response I can have? Should I be silent? Whatever it is, is there something different I can do that will get me closer to achieving my Purpose?" The key was keeping that Purpose foremost in their minds and letting it inform every choice they made.

Once they got clear on the Purpose, we dove into their Context: "Okay, your Purpose is to get our freedom back. But right now we've determined that the unconscious or default Context you're holding is, *We hate these guys, they're horrible and untrustworthy; they screwed us.* We already agreed that, if you go into the negotiation holding to this Context, you are not very likely to be successful in achieving your Purpose of getting our freedom back, right?"

"Right."

"What is the Context you need to hold to achieve your Purpose?" What Lenny initially came up with was that they needed to remain calm, and Gina was quickly in agreement. They weren't currently in the space of remaining calm, but they realized that if they could remain calm and not reactive, then that would empower them.

They were also very impatient. They wanted out *now*. Interestingly, although Lenny was angrier and they were both impatient, Gina was the one who was most impatient and kept repeating, "I just can't wait to have my life back!" We determined that this impatience could really cost them. Not that they didn't want to expedite things, but if they were really impatient and they pushed it too hard, then they could either seem desperate, or they could push things to litigation too quickly. The only reason they really wanted out was because they were fed up. There was no inherent time deadline. Once we discussed it, they realized that getting their freedom back was more important than accomplishing that goal by some artificially imposed deadline, so they added the Context of being patient to their list.

Then they realized the other thing they needed to be was collaborative, which was a tough one for them to get to because these were people they had already emotionally dismissed and written off. They hated them, didn't trust them, and barely could stand to be in a room with them. It's often not easy to get people to be collaborative even in a more positive deal-negotiating context, but if you are negotiating in the face of a dispute and a broken business relationship, it's certainly a lot tougher for people to stay collaborative.

But this particular scenario demanded a level of collaboration from our side, despite the mistrust and hard feelings, because to get to a deal there were many moving pieces that had to be taken into account. Not only did they want to get a deal, but they also needed cooperation from their soon-to-be former colleagues to provide a smooth transition for their clients. Even if Lenny and Gina could negotiate a satisfactory deal for themselves and their partners, if it left things in a mess as far as moving their client accounts was concerned, then it would have hurt their clients. They cared about their clients, not simply as a matter of good business but because they genuinely cared about the clients' welfare. Lenny and Gina realized that both in the negotiation itself and in the energy of it going forward, it was important to be collaborative.

So they prepared themselves to be calm, patient, and collaborative. But as they examined it, they realized that there was something missing because as important as those qualities were, they were up against tough negotiators, sophisticated businesspeople who had likely not done the necessary work to become as connected or evolved. These opponents might be reactionary. Lenny said, "Those three words work for me, but we're not quite there. I know these guys, and I don't want to get taken advantage of. It feels a little soft." What was missing from their Context that could protect them and be empowering?

I'm sometimes asked how best to narrow down the potential list of words you can use to get to the core Context; most of us have no trouble coming up with a lot of words, but having the *right* words is paramount. As I have said, I stay away from offering more suggestions than are absolutely necessary because these words must be personal in order to resonate, and I don't want to limit my clients' thinking. This is not a process you can shortcut. Every situation is different.

This is not a process you can shortcut.

I will tell you, though, some common characteristics of words that people have come up with that have been successful for them. First, they're always positive. It's not useful to have a Context or a Purpose that comes from a negative place. You could have a Purpose that says, "I want to beat those jerks." That's a Purpose, but the Purposes that are effective and the Contexts that are effective come from a positive and empowering place.

If you were a fly on the wall for our discussion on this last missing piece, it derived from, "Hey listen, these guys are tough negotiators. We can't back down from those guys. We can't be weak. We can't let them think we're pushovers." They said things like, "We have to be aggressive." We discarded words like "aggressive" and "pushover" because they had a negative or reactive energy to them, which is what eventually brought them to "firm," a word they viewed positively. It wasn't a reactive word. It wasn't a negative word. It was not weak. For some people, "strong" might have been the right word: for them, "strong" had some aggressive connotations that still had some charge in them. "Firm" was a place where they could stand and achieve those same results and get the same message across, but it came from a centered place for them. When we were at that stage of the work, I was helping them, more or less offering up words. I suggested "firm" when "strong" was not quite there for them, and they simultaneously jumped on it and said, "Yes, that's it!" That's what you want to get to, that "aha!" moment. When people get their Purpose and their Context, they know it: "That's it." It's not intellectual—it's at a gut level. So Gina and Lenny's Context became *firm, calm, patient,* and *collaborative.*

The key question to ask when you're creating a Context is, if you hold that Context, does it create the best likelihood of you achieving your Purpose? In their case, that Purpose was to get our freedom back. They thought it through and decided that the Context they'd created, that constellation of powerful words and ideas, put them in the best position to achieve that Purpose. That four-word Context spoke to them. It was something that they were excited about. It was something they could reconnect to in the tough times of negotiation.

In addition to saying to themselves, "Is this next action I'm about to do or say going to move me closer to or further away from achieving my Purpose?" they could also say, "Okay, in this moment, am I being firm, calm, patient, and collaborative or not?"

When you're going through this process and ask yourself this question, if the answer is "no," then you need to shift. In the heat of things, it's easy to lose your focus and potentially your control along with it, but you must always stay in that Context or get back into it as quickly as possible if you become disconnected. If, in the course of the negotiation, you can feel that you're getting thrown off, take a break. Go outside. Take a breath. Say you've got to go to the restroom or have to make a phone call or whatever you can come up with, and reconnect. Take that time alone to revisit your CPR.

I always encourage people to memorize their CPRs, at least the Context and the Purpose, but also to bring a copy with them because if they really get thrown off and can't remember it, then they'll have a copy they can refer to, either during a break or discretely in the room.

So we had the Context and Purpose. I then discussed with Lenny and Gina the specifics of the Results they wanted to get out of the negotiation. They had a list of outcomes that they wanted. What we did in this particular situation was to create a draft separation agreement that outlined the terms of the deal that they wanted. We knew it would be negotiated, but we decided to just make it real. This is what we want in the form of the legal agreement that we hope to get signed.

One of their Results was that they'd sign a separation agreement by a certain date. We also needed a standstill agreement so that, in the event the negotiations broke down, we'd get to file the first lawsuit. It was important to us, with regard to our plan B, that we be the plaintiff, meaning we get to shoot first. A standstill agreement says, "We won't sue each other while we're negotiating." Until one of the parties gives notice that the negotiation has broken down, nobody can sue each other. It gives both sides comfort, and getting that standstill agreement signed was a key objective. They also wanted to negotiate a joint press release so that what was put out in the industry was uniform and the messaging was aligned.

They wanted to maintain amicable relationships with these guys that they hated because, as I said before, it was important that the clients' transition went smoothly so that their clients wouldn't be alienated through this process. And they didn't want to pay above a certain amount of money; they had a specific figure in mind for which they were willing to cut a check.

The Results contained some items that were strictly quantitative, like how much they wanted to pay, and others that were binary, like whether or not a standstill agreement was signed. But then there were also things that were qualitative, like whether they were maintaining an amicable relationship or not.

LENNY AND GINA'S CPR

CONTEXT
Firm, Calm, Patient, and Collaborative

PURPOSE
To get our freedom back.

RESULTS
1. Sign a separation agreement with the deal terms set forth in the draft we prepared by x date.
2. Sign standstill agreement at first negotiating session.
3. Schedule the second negotiating session.
4. Maintain an amicable relationship with the y company executives.

Then, in preparation for the face-to-face meetings, we did some role-playing. It's great to do the CPR and say, "Okay, we're ready to go in there." But what happens once you're in the heat of negotiation? How well will you use the CPR to maintain CDE when you're under pressure? As Mike Tyson says, "Everyone has a plan until they get punched in the mouth." So we role-played these negotiations several times, where I played the roles of some of the players on the other side. I purposely said and did things that I knew were likely to trigger Lenny and Gina. It's interesting; you would think in a role-play that people would know and remember that it's just role-playing, and they wouldn't actually get triggered—but in my experience, when you're role-playing, it often gets real, and it certainly did this time.

As we did the role-playing exercise, when they got triggered or answered in a way that I thought wasn't moving them toward their Purpose and intended Results, or if they weren't holding their

Context, I would stop the exercise, drop out of character, and talk them through it. Sometimes I would keep it going, and I'd make notes as we went along and we'd debrief afterward.

I'd say, "When I said x in role-playing the CEO of the other side and you said y, let's look at that in hindsight. Do you think that really moved us toward your Purpose? Were you holding your Context there?" They had the opportunity to see and analyze where they'd done that successfully and where they hadn't. We went through this exercise four or five times, until we agreed that they'd reached a level of confidence and self-awareness adequate to prepare them to withstand being triggered. They had done the work to gain Clarity, Detachment, and Equilibrium and to create a powerful CPR.

Fast-forward, and it was time for the negotiations to begin. Gina and Lenny flew to Dallas for the meeting. We had an attorney sitting at the courthouse, prepared to file the lawsuit if things didn't go well. For all we knew, the other side had lawyers sitting in a courthouse in a different state ready to file a lawsuit as well. The client had instructions to text the word "file" to us if things went bad—so that we could file first. My team and I were at my office waiting, trying to get other work done but really sitting on the edges of our desk chairs wondering how things were going.

Well, we didn't receive a text saying, "file," so that was a good sign. Eventually, Gina texted that things went pretty well and that they would call as soon as they left the building. When they called us, they reported that they have an agreement to sign the standstill, that all parties have agreed to work toward a negotiated exit deal, and they have scheduled their next negotiating session. Good results for the first session!

After that first session, it took several months, a few more direct client negotiating sessions, and a lot of input and negotiations between the attorneys as well to settle the deal. It was back and forth and featured some compromise, but ultimately my clients ended up getting what they wanted and almost all of their intended Results. Most importantly, they got their freedom back, which was their Purpose. It cost them a few more dollars than they'd hoped to pay but not more than their bottom line; they were able to stay within their range. The transition of their clients was relatively smooth and cooperative, and they moved on to better places. They were free. Now, some years later, Lenny and Gina are very happy. There is no question in my mind that they wouldn't have gotten that result without going through the CPR process and coming to the bargaining table with that level of Clarity, Detachment, and Equilibrium.

Now, let's dig into how the CPR process can work for you.

CHAPTER SEVEN

BRINGING THE CPR PROCESS TO YOUR NEGOTIATIONS AND BEYOND

A s you learned in the previous chapter, CPR stands for the three parts of the internal preparation framework: Context, Purpose, and Results.

The Context is who you need to be in order to achieve your objectives. The Context is really a "being" discussion and not about a "why." It's not about doing anything. It's about who you are when you walk into that room. What is your state of being? We've talked in other places in the book about how if your state of being is fear, scarcity, reaction, or anger, then it is not going to be very useful. Whether you call it "state of being" or "ground of being" or Context, the question to ask yourself at every step of the negotiation is, *Who am I being right now, and does it support my success in this negotiation?*

The Purpose is the "why." In the example I used in the previous chapter, the "why" for my client was to get their freedom back. Your "why" might be to get a raise in a situation where you'll have to negotiate with your boss. Your "why" could be to expand your business through a distribution deal or a marketing deal. Your "why" could be to enter into a phenomenal business partnership that will allow you to focus on your highest and best use areas. The true "why" is often even deeper than these examples.

Whatever your specific desired goal is, stripped down to its most precise components, is your Purpose. Here's the key thing to remember in drafting your Purpose and your Context: you want to keep these things brief. In the example in the previous chapter, my clients' "why" was to get their freedom back, and the phrase "Get our freedom back" is very simple, easy to remember, and gets to the core of it. Your Purpose shouldn't be a paragraph, just a brief phrase or a sentence at most. Why so limited in length?

First of all, I want you to be able to memorize it. Second of all, and even more important, I want you to get to the core of what your "why" is. Usually if you use more words, you're not getting to the core. There's a famous anecdote about President Woodrow Wilson being asked how long it took him to prepare a speech. He replied, "It depends. If I am to speak ten minutes, I need a week for preparation; if fifteen minutes, three days; if half an hour, two days; if an hour, I am ready now."

In other words, to do less takes more time because it requires more thought to drill down. You can start out with a paragraph, but then you have to whittle it down to its core. What's the essence of that paragraph? With enough attention, you can always get it down to a phrase or a sentence. Keeping it that brief forces you to go through the work required to boil your "why" down to its quintessence and compels you to define for yourself what it is you're genuinely after.

Even in the example I gave of somebody going in to negotiate a raise, the Purpose could be to get a raise. But, more likely, in working with that person, I would ask, "What is it that you really want?" A great way to dig down to that core purpose is to keep asking why: Why do you want to get a raise? Why does a raise matter?

> **Keeping it that brief forces you to go through the work required to boil your "why" down to its quintessence and compels you to define for yourself what it is you're genuinely after.**

"Well, my kids are a few years away from college. I'll need the money to pay for college." We're digging a little deeper. That's a little more motivating.

"Why is that important to you?"

"It's super important that my kid can get educated," or, "I didn't have the opportunity to go to college. It's important that she does." Now, we're at the crux of why that raise is important; your child's future depends on you getting it.

That said, you can always ask another "why." There's a point at which you need to stop, and in the prior example, maybe we've reached it. "My purpose is to assure that my daughter has the opportunity to go to college that I didn't have." How much more powerful is that than a Purpose that simply says, "My purpose is to get a raise"?

There is a wonderful technique called the *5 Whys* that was developed by Sakichi Toyoda and used within the Toyota Motor Corporation during the evolution of its manufacturing methodologies. In this exercise, you ask "Why?" five times, using the answer to the previous question as the basis for the next question. This technique is useful in negotiating preparation as well to help determine your Purpose. In the example I gave, I only asked two whys, but it often takes five to get to the deeper truth. When I do this exercise with people, a lot of times the initial Purpose statements are rather superficial. I don't mean that as a criticism, it's just where people start. When "my Purpose is to get a raise" turns into "my Purpose is to assure that my daughter has the opportunity to go to college that I didn't have," that's powerful. That's motivating. That's something you can stay connected to if you end up in a tough negotiation with your boss. It's not about just wanting more money.

We need to get down to that level of Purpose. We want to keep it simple; if we wrote a whole paragraph on why it was important to send a kid to college, I think that would be less powerful than if that purpose is, "My purpose is to assure that my daughter has the opportunity to go to college that I didn't have." That's an easy-to-remember, brief sentence that says everything important.

When it comes to Context, some people like to state their Context as either a sentence or a phrase as well. That's fine, since this is really about what works for and resonates with you—the person who is doing the CPR. For myself, I generally find that using a list of words is most powerful and effective—just three or four of them, similar to the example I gave in the last chapter where my clients chose "firm, calm, patient, and collaborative." There's power in those words' simplicity and directness. Whether it is a list or words for you or a phrase or sentence, the important thing is to dig deep, get to the essence, and keep it brief.

When you're digging, you may initially come up with numerous different ideas, but getting to the core can take a while, and you really can't rush it. For instance, those clients got pretty quickly to the certainty that they needed to be calm. "Patient" was another one that they got to relatively quickly. "Collaborative" took a while to get to, as did "firm." Searching for the word they needed that wouldn't be reactionary, wouldn't be triggered, but would still keep them from being patsies or weak, took a while, but ultimately that work proved to be invaluable to them. On both Context and Purpose, there's just no substitute for putting whatever time is required to properly define them in your own terms. They have to resonate for *you*.

Of course, if you're going to the flea market and negotiating the price on the used lawnmower with the fellow at the stand, I'm not saying you have to go off and spend hours figuring out your Context and Purpose—but it's actually not a bad thing to do a quick CPR just as practice, to get yourself into the habit. Because I have used this methodology so often, I find that although I may not be doing the full CPR process on less-important negotiations, those concepts remain present with me. Even in small negotiations, they're somewhere in there, whether or not I've fully articulated them on paper.

It's clear that in any significant negotiation—a multimillion-dollar deal, a billion-dollar deal, or even just getting that raise or negotiating a key strategic alliance, business partnership, or contract—you're going to want to invest the time commensurate with the importance of the outcome of that deal to you. But even when it's something like your kid not having been admitted into a private school, where you're going in to meet with and convince the admissions officer to let her in, that too is a negotiation in which you'll have greater success if you apply these teachings and spend the time to get clear on your Context and Purpose. It's a worthy investment to make for any issue that has meaningful stakes attached to it.

Finally, the "R" stands for "Results," the practical results, the intended results. They're the specific, measurable outcomes of your efforts: i.e., "I want x amount in a raise, I want it to start on this date," or "I want to sell my company for at least y dollars," or "I want my three key employees to be hired by the buyer," or "I want my payments to be z over a specific number of years," or "I want to make sure my clients are well taken care of and that we do a joint announcement." The Results vary, depending on what you're negotiating, but those are the kinds of specific, measurable Results we're talking about here. Being completely clear about your desired Results is fundamental to the process and your ultimate success.

An interesting point on CPR is that you can do the CPR for the overall negotiation, and then you can additionally do a separate CPR for each negotiating session. Whether you do just one overall CPR or the usefulness of additional CPRs for each session depends on the size and flow of the negotiation. If it's a big enough deal, you might have five to ten negotiating sessions. You can prepare yourself for each of them individually: "Here's my overall CPR, but now I have a CPR for this particular session."

In this multiple CPR approach, your Context will stay the same, since the Context is something you must hold for the entire negotiation process. The Purpose, too—the overall purpose—is going to stay the same, but you may have a sort of subpurpose for each particular negotiating session.

When you're preparing sub-CPRs, the overall Results don't change, either. You may have a list of fifteen Results that you want in the overall negotiation, but in session number one, the Results you want to achieve will only be three or four of those. You're going to knock those off in that session and save the rest for later. And then, you may add Results that are applicable specifically to that session only—for example, making sure you get the next negotiation session scheduled.

Another great thing about CPR is that it works whether you're the big, brawny sumo wrestler or the little guy in the ring. With the other kinds of postures—table banging and so forth—that we've discussed, there are always different tactics and techniques that may "work," depending on your leverage point. This works no matter who you are. I don't mean to suggest, of course, that it's going to guarantee you'll get everything you want. Leverage does matter. That said, no matter where you are on the leverage spectrum, CPR will increase your chances significantly of having a more successful negotiation.

What it will also do is to help you get clear as to what you need to achieve in the negotiation to move forward—the Clarity part of CDE. If you're clear on what your Context, Purpose, and Results are and you get to a point in the negotiation where it's evident that you're not going to achieve your Purpose, you will be able to see that and respond appropriately, rather than out of ego or anger. So CPR supports the Equilibrium part of CDE, as well.

With CPR, you increase your chances of being successful significantly, but it also supports you in getting Clarity more quickly on whether the negotiations are not going to allow you to achieve your Purpose and Results. In the example I gave in the previous chapter, had my clients gotten to the point where they were clear that they would not be able to get their freedom back, they would have texted our guy sitting at the courthouse and said, "file," and we would have filed that lawsuit. They would have been in a litigation (their BATNA), which wouldn't have been a great result, but it was much better having that Clarity than if they had ended up in a situation where the other side sued them first in a less-favorable jurisdiction. So, using this tool, you will have a clearer understanding of when you need to move to your plan B, your alternative. Here, CPR is supporting the Detachment part of CDE.

As you can see, CPR is one of the core frameworks on which the practical application of a lot of my training and teaching is based. It really is just a tool, though, albeit a powerful tool. The real challenge is to attain and maintain your CDE—Clarity, Detachment, and Equilibrium—in whatever way you can with or without using CPR.

As you can see, CPR is one of the core frameworks on which the practical application of a lot of my training and teaching is based. It really is just a tool, though, albeit a powerful tool. The real challenge is to attain and maintain your CDE—Clarity, Detachment, and Equilibrium—in whatever way you can with or without using CPR.

With CPR, though, you get a huge bonus that goes beyond negotiating. CPR is a tool that can be used not only in those kinds of interactions but also in many other areas in your life. If you're having a challenge in your relationship, you can do a CPR for your relationship that you and your partner can come to jointly or separately, and create a shared Context, Purpose, and Results you want to achieve in the relationship. You can even do one around your health, if you aren't happy with its current state and need to define your goals and objectives, and the purpose and context that underlie them, in a way that will make them achievable.

You can see how doing a CPR around other areas of your life could help you get clarity: creating a powerful Context, a powerful "why"—a Purpose—and then using these to create some intended Results can really make a difference. I think this is one of the reasons people make and quickly break New Year's resolutions; they don't stick to them, because really what they're doing in making those New Year's resolutions is simply stating the hoped-for results: "I'm going to lose thirty pounds," "I'm going to exercise three times a week," "I'm going to make more money." But where the real work is done is, as we've seen, on the Context and the Purpose. If you apply that in other areas of your life, whether in business, whether in health, whether with family or with your kids—if you do that work to get clear and come from a powerful Context and Purpose, then you are much more likely to achieve the Results you want.

Even personal finances can be approached in this way. Say you're unhappy with the amount of money you're making or saving. If you start with "I have to spend less," or "I have to go on a budget," that's coming from a place of obligation and limitation, and it has a negative quality. It is built on past failures and frustrations, and it doesn't come from a powerful place on which you can stand, so you're not likely to be successful at it.

But what if you bring a powerful Context around what's driving you to improve your finances? Maybe you have a young child, and you're really worried about providing for your family. Maybe you just have bigger aspirations for what you want to do and the kind of life you want to have; you want to travel, or you want to live in a nicer house. Maybe you want to earn money because you want to make a bigger difference in the world, and you want to be able to use that money to make a positive impact.

If you can connect it to that powerful underlying reason—if your child's welfare for instance is the "why," the Purpose for which you're making money—then that's going to be much more compelling than something less resonant, such as "I spend too much." If you're not achieving the results you want at the time, then your Context is probably not powerful enough and clear enough to be a basis for you to be successful. If your Purpose is to make a better life for your children and you have a Context that comes from love, contribution, sharing, accountability, being a great father or mother—whatever it is for you—then that's a much more powerful place to come from than "I don't make enough money, I'm a failure, I'm underpaid."

What if you have a challenging relationship with a parent and you don't feel good when you're with them because you're always fighting? What would it be like to step back and create a CPR for yourself for that relationship? Or in your relationship with your teenaged children? Based upon the experience of many who have successfully used this tool, I know that it can work for you in those potentially emotionally fraught situations, too, not just in negotiations.

One of the big messages for me is that as human beings in negotiation, and in many other areas of life, we tend to spend more time on the external, whether it's the other people or the "to-dos"; we focus on the actions. We have a tendency not to want to spend time on the internal work that needs to be done to give us the best chance for success. I've given pretty clear illustrations of that on how that impacts negotiation, but it also impacts other parts of your life.

For instance, when I talked about personal finances, you could try to resolve the personal finance issue by going out and getting a second job, right? But if your relationship to your money isn't a healthy one, then that's probably either not going to work, or it's going to be a huge burden, and you're going to continue to struggle along. So I think the bigger message I'd like you to take from this is to be willing to do the internal work. There's a classic quote by the

Persian poet Rumi, which says, "Yesterday I was clever, so I wanted to change the world. Today I am wise, so I am changing myself."

With the understanding that CDE brings, the other things you have learned in this book, and the CPR framework, I am confident that you can change how you deal with others—in business, in your personal relations, and even with yourself in a way that is more honest, more fruitful, and far more positive. You can become an authentic negotiator, be authentic in your business, and live an authentic life. I say this with confidence not only based upon the experience of helping others for more than thirty years but also from my own personal journey.

> "Yesterday I was clever, so I wanted to change the world. Today I am wise, so I am changing myself."

In the introduction, I said my real test of those teachings came in 2008, and I promised to share that story. So here it is. You remember a little something called the Great Recession, right? Well, the Great Recession hit my businesses extremely hard, as, of course, it did so many others. I'm a deal guy, and there were no deals going on, and day-to-day corporate and contract work dried up as clients were significantly impacted and nobody was starting new businesses. My revenue dropped $30K, $40K, $50K per month. On top of that, I had clients who owed me a lot of money go out of business and not pay their bills. Only several years before, I had built out a new office and had a loan I was paying down from that. I had invested in a couple of real estate investment funds that a partner and I had created, and my money and the money we raised from investors was at significant risk. In fact, we ended up losing two of our buildings to foreclosure. A weekend lake home that I owned was financially under water and causing a severe financial strain and, like so many, I was slow to cut personnel and overhead.

I ended up about $325K in debt (not counting the lake house mortgages) and was another $50K in the hole in terms of the value of the lake house vs. the mortgage amounts. For a period of time, my wife and I gave up our apartment and slept in my office on an air mattress. Thankfully, the office had a shower. I was getting creditor calls daily. I couldn't believe that I was in this position at that point of my life and career. Several of my close friends and advisors recommended that I file for bankruptcy or, at least, short sale the lake house.

I searched deep inside and knew I couldn't declare bankruptcy or walk away from the lake house or any of my other debts (even those that were through my businesses and not personally guaranteed) and stay true to who I am. I had made commitments, and it was my integrity, honor, reputation, and sense of self that was at stake. Once I was clear on that, there was only one thing left to do. Negotiate. Authentically.

There was a lot of negotiating necessary with a lot of different people and entities—trade creditors, landlords, vendors, banks, credit card companies—and this became the ultimate test of my CDE negotiating philosophy, approach, and framework. Not a test of whether or not CDE worked; I already had many years of proof that it did. It was a test, instead, of whether—under the worst circumstances I had ever experienced in business and the extreme level of stress and pressure I was feeling—I could actually practice what I preached.

You see, as you now know from reading this far, I had been teaching and preaching that great negotiating is not about the tactics, techniques, and countertactics that many books and trainings focus on (some of which are manipulative and others of which are okay but not the core of great negotiating) but instead required significant and deep inner work to achieve a certain state of being in which you can connect to and maintain the core framework—CDE. My understanding of what it takes to achieve and maintain CDE had never been as deeply tested as during that time.

I spent many hours of the following weeks and months getting 100 percent clarity on what I could and could not do in terms of every lender and creditor to whom I owed money and every vendor whose services I continued to need. I also looked at every expense, business and personal, and my commitments to my family and employees. I did the deep internal work to get clarity on what would be in integrity for me—what was consistent with my own truth and what negotiating approach that dictated. I created a CPR for the situation and each of the important negotiations.

Here is the initial overall CPR that I created:

CONTEXT
Word, Transparency, Learning, and Joy

PURPOSE
To joyfully honor all of my commitments in full integrity without exception while taking care of my family, supporting my employees, and serving my clients.

RESULTS
1. Pay all debts in full within five years.
2. Negotiate payment plans with total monthly payments of not more than $3K/mo. to start.
3. Be in regular communication with all creditors and vendors—return every call, and reply to every email.
4. Be open, honest, and transparent in all communications.
5. Pay all newly incurred bills timely (business and personal).
6. Fully fund every payroll.
7. Maintain my good credit rating.
8. Maintain access to my bank line of credit without redrawing on it/line of credit not called.
9. Enjoy life.

After getting to a place of Clarity and creating the CPR, I was able to be Detached to the outcome of any given negotiation. I knew what would work for me and what wouldn't—not from a place of ego or anger or being right but from a place of Clarity. I was willing to trust that everything would work out whether or not that particular negotiating session ended the way I wanted. I also worked to stay calm and centered—maintain my Equilibrium—in every negotiation, despite extreme pressure, threats, and accusations from collection companies and the like. Although I did well in maintaining my Equilibrium overall, I wasn't always 100 percent successful and at times needed to reconnect and get back to my center after allowing myself to get thrown off.

It was hard—very hard. At every step of the way, my negotiating philosophy, commitment to my teachings, and ability to follow them were tested. But by using the guidelines I have offered in this book, I ended up successfully negotiating payment plans with every creditor by mid-2009 and paid back every dollar (which was my commitment) within five years, while increasing my retirement savings by over $200K and, after the first year, being able to live a comfortable lifestyle. It took another two years to divest all of the properties in the real estate investment funds—including successfully negotiating to receive a payment from the lender of one of the properties in foreclosure—and return to our investors a much higher percentage of their invested capital than seemed possible during the Great Recession. I sold the lake house and funded the full deficit of the excess of the mortgage loans above the sale price from my savings. Despite it being one of the most challenging times of my life, I was able to maintain my joy more than you would think and, certainly, more than I would have been able to if it had not been in my CPR.

Today, all of my business and personal relationships from that time and my reputation remain intact, I still have my bank credit line available, I am business and personally debt free (other than a car loan on a car that has more than $4,000 in value above the loan), I maintain a credit score above 800, and most importantly, I held to my values and maintained my integrity. All of which was made possible by practicing what I preached and following what I have taught you in this book.

I wish you much success in your negotiations and hope this book plays a part in that success.

IN CLOSING

I am a professional negotiator. People hire me to negotiate everything from small to very large corporate deals to various types of disputes and for other tough negotiating situations, mostly in the realm of business. I also facilitate negotiating trainings for companies and individuals, do negotiating consulting, and speak on Authentic Negotiating. If somebody has a particular negotiating situation, I can either negotiate it for them or I can help them in the background—offering them advice and training on how they handle it. I do much of this through my speaking, training, and consulting firm, Authentic Enterprises, LLC (www.authenticenterprises.com), the mission of which is to inspire authenticity in business. The main vehicle to achieve this mission is the Authentic Business Academy, which in addition to Authentic Negotiating includes entrepreneurial and corporate training workshops on authentic deal making, building authentic business relationships, and authentic conversations about difference. I speak on those topics as well.

In addition to that, I have my law firm, Kupfer & Associates, PLLC (www.kupferlaw.com), through which my team and I work with companies during their entire lifecycle from start-up through exit, and, of course, negotiating and deal making is a huge part of that. I love helping people achieve their business goals while supporting them to run authentic businesses and live authentic lives. How do we strategize to make that possible, and what kind of deals do we need to cut? What kind of relationships do we need to establish, how do we negotiate those relationships and deals, and then how do we make them successful while making sure everything we do is true to who we are?

Fundamentally, I believe in human potential. Every one of us on this planet, no matter what our circumstances, has within us the power to have success in our lives. That applies to anything we put our minds to, including being successful negotiators but also to being successful in business, relationships, and any other realm. Many people lose their positive outlooks about their potential; perhaps past failures color their sense of their own value and ability, or they just don't see the way to improve. I believe that the truth lies within. If we have the courage to connect to it, trust it, follow it, and take massive action based upon it, we will be successful.

Bringing that same understanding and energy into negotiations substantially increases the chances of your success there as well. If we can support or serve you in any way, please reach out. My team and I would be honored to work with you.